The Complete Illustrated
LABRADOR

The Complete Illustrated
LABRADOR

Edited by
Joe and Liz Cartledge

With contributions by

MICHAEL BOOTHROYD
JOE CARTLEDGE
LIZ CARTLEDGE
JO COULSON
JOHN HOLMES
BETTY PENN-BULL
MICHAEL STOCKMAN
ANN WYNYARD

Ebury Press · London

Sally Anne Thompson

First published 1974
by Ebury Press
Chestergate House, Vauxhall Bridge Road
London SW1V 1HF

© J. H. Cartledge 1974

All rights reserved. No part of this publication may be reproduced, stored in a retrieval system, or transmitted in any form or by any means, electronic, mechanical, photocopying, recording or otherwise, without the prior permission of the copyright owner.

ISBN 0 85223 046 X

Imperial Public Library
Imperial, Texas

Photoset in Great Britain by
Typesetting Services Ltd, Glasgow
and printed and bound by
Interlitho s.p.a., Milan, Italy

Contents

1 The Labrador as a Pet	*page 8*
2 Living with your Labrador	*26*
3 History of the Labrador Retriever	*38*
4 Training	*48*
5 Breeding	*76*
6 The Labrador in the Field	*100*
7 The Labrador as Guide Dog for the Blind	*116*
8 Common Illnesses	*120*
9 Kennel Club Breed Standard	*134*
Index	*136*

The Editors

JOE CARTLEDGE
It would be right to say that Joe Cartledge has been concerned with pedigree dogs and dog shows all his life. Before the First World War and between the two wars his uncle, the late Arthur Cartledge, was one of the foremost dog handlers in Britain and in the United States. It was in these surroundings and environment that Joe developed his love for the dog game. Except for his years in the services in the Second World War dogs have been his whole life, first as a boy with his uncle, and then as kennelman with the world famous Crackley Terrier Kennels. In 1949 he started his own kennels and handled dogs for many of the top people in the dog world throughout the fifties, winning championships in eleven different breeds, including Dog of the Year award on two occasions, and Best in Show with an Airedale Terrier at Cruft's, the world's most important dog show, in 1961. He retired from handling at the end of 1961 as he found that, with the handling of dogs both here and on the Continent, his writing and judging both in Britain and abroad, he was becoming too diversified. He now judges almost every week in Britain, and has judged in Hong Kong, Ceylon, Singapore, Malaysia, Australia, New Zealand, Rhodesia, Zambia, The Republic of South Africa, Brazil, Argentina, Uruguay, Finland, Sweden, Norway, Denmark, Italy, Germany, Switzerland and Holland. He contributes a weekly column in *Dog World,* the top weekly paper devoted to pedigree dogs. He is Chairman of Ryslip Kennels Ltd., and of Ryslip Livestock Shipping Company. He edits and publishes the *Dog Directory* and *Dog Diary*.

LIZ CARTLEDGE
Although young in years, Liz, like her husband, has also spent her entire life with dogs. She was born in Gothenburg, Sweden, to parents who were both concerned with the exhibiting and training of dogs, mainly Dobermanns and Boxers. She came to England first in 1964 as a kennel student with the Dreymin Kennels of Beagles, Bassets and Corgis. Later, and until her marriage, she was on the editorial staff of *Dog World*. A dog judge herself, she travels the world as secretary to her husband, one of the busiest judges in the world today.

1 The Labrador as a Pet

BY ANN WYNYARD

So you are considering having a Labrador puppy? I won't question your choice, because in my opinion the Labrador Retriever is one of the most versatile of all breeds, but I will ask you your motives, for Labradors don't suit everyone. It is never a good idea to follow fashion blindly without first finding out whether a particular breed of dog is the one that can best adapt to you and your environment.

It is true that Labradors are found in all walks of life—on the Royal grouse moors, in humble cottages, doing police work (mainly drug detection), working as guide dogs for blind people, and so on. They can make the most devoted of companions, intelligent, brave and humorous. What a Labrador should *not* be is a useless ornament, a status symbol or a guard dog.

Points to consider are that a growing Labrador puppy will drink a pint of milk a day and eat three-quarters of a pound of meat; it will require, in all weathers, at least two good walks of not less than a mile each, one of them free off the lead; it needs either suitable kennel accommodation with a run, or else a large enough house to prevent its tail sweeping things off tables; it will require some kind of mental stimulation, as it was never designed to be a vegetable. Read in another chapter in this book about the origins of the breed, and you will see that the Labrador is a dog bred for intelligence and brains. To shut one up alone all day in house or kennel is to ask for trouble. Neither the breed nor the individual dog will be to blame, but the thoughtless purchaser, who should either have a cat or a guinea-pig—or no animal at all!

So, make sure that your garden has a reasonable amount of room for a young and boisterous puppy to let off steam, that it can be made dog-proof (this is of vital importance, as male Labradors are often great wanderers), that your pocket is deep enough to cope with the feeding costs and occasional veterinary bills, and above all that at least one member of your family is available to exercise the dog in rain or shine for about two hours daily.

Now to more detailed facts. The Labrador Retriever

comes in three colours—liver (milk-chocolate brown), black and yellow. Let me say here, please, once and for all, that there is no such breed as a *golden* Labrador. The word 'yellow' covers all the shades ranging from pale Devonshire cream to deep fox red, including all the golds, oranges and lemon-yellows in between. The rarest to breed and hardest to find is probably the liver-coloured Labrador.

The real Labrador temperament should be denoted by the dog's typical expression of intelligence and kindness—though it is unfortunately true that in many countries of the world the Labrador has been bought and bred for mass production, and in some cases scant attention has been paid to temperament; unless this tendency is watched, it could be the downfall of one of the most wonderful breeds we have.

If Labradors are brought up with children and with other dogs they are generally very good, but it might be a little hard to expect an older Labrador to put up with children tormenting or teasing him—but then, a dog should never have to put up with too much of this treatment.

Bitches probably make more placid pets, with less inclination to wander, except when they are in season. If you cannot contend with the local Romeos and have no desire to breed from your bitch, you can of course have her spayed. I still don't like the idea of having any male dog castrated, and having always had a preference for Labrador males (who don't have the inconvenient habit of coming on heat in the shooting season), I have found that if they are mentally occupied and well exercised they have no desire to stray and wander, though some Labrador males can be over-sexed.

Buying Your Puppy
When you start to look at litters of puppies, do be prepared to go a little beyond your own doorstep. There are two weekly dog papers, *Dog World* and *Our Dogs* (obtainable through any newsagent), which contain 'stock for sale' advertisements. In the *Dog Directory* (published yearly, and available on most bookstalls, or directly from

The Labrador as a Pet : 11

the publishers at Binfield Park, Bracknell, Berkshire) are listed reputable breeders up and down the country who usually have puppies available. Names and addresses can also be obtained from Dog Breeders Associates (1 Clarges Street, Piccadilly, London W1Y 8AB). Incidentally, let me say here that any holder of a prefix or affix can advertise in the *Kennel Gazette* (obtainable from the Kennel Club) for a small payment; it does not mean that these are the names of the top breeders—though obviously these may be included. Your local veterinary surgeons could also help you with advice on local breeders; and if necessary, you can ask the RSPCA or the police station for the nearest vet's name and address.

Much as I hate to say this, if you buy 'that doggie in the window', however appealing, you will have no idea of its background or breeding just from the pedigree. That is why I stress buying from a breeder, so that you can at

least see the dam and the conditions the puppy has come from. And of course any breeder worth his salt will give advice and help if needed.

Having got your list of breeders, go and see at least two litters before making up your mind, and if you are not happy with those two, then go and see some more. You are buying what you hope will be a companion for the next ten or twelve years or more—exactly how long the dog will eventually live depends to a large extent on your care.

These are basic points to remember when you visit a breeder:

(*a*) Note the cleanliness of the kennels and surroundings.

(*b*) Don't be content to see just one puppy, brought into a room for your inspection; note the temperament of the mother, as well as her litter's behaviour.

(*c*) Ask to see the copy of the puppy's pedigree and make sure that it is not too closely inbred. On the other hand, don't be dazzled by advertisements which quote number of champions in the pedigree.

(*d*) Ask to see the father if available (though this will not often be the case, as people travel miles to mate their bitches to suitable dogs).

(*e*) See that the puppies look healthy, with bright eyes, not weeping or encrusted, that their coats are not staring, with patches of bare skin, that they have good bone and substance, and no pot bellies, denoting worms. Look at the skin on the stomach and make sure they don't have an umbilical (naval) hernia, nor any spots and sores on the soft skin. Nor should the puppies smell of anything other than milk and biscuits.

Of course, if you want a show puppy, then you must go to kennels which have a good reputation in the show ring, and the sire or dam—preferably both—should have a long list of wins. To some extent a novice must rely upon the aid of the breeder, but remember, even the top breeders admit that with the best will in the world they can't always pick out a champion from the nest. So much can go wrong in the six months from birth until a dog is eligible for the

show ring. However, in this chapter I am assuming you want a pet.

When you make your final choice, temperament should come very high on the list. The impression should be that of a gay, well-balanced puppy, frightened of nothing. Don't pick out that shivering puppy who sits back quaking while the rest of the litter reveal themselves as boisterous extroverts. Choose one which has a nice square body, deep in the chest, with good solid bone, a square head with good proportion of muzzle to skull, defined stop, kind eyes, neither too dark nor too light (hazel ones with plenty of expression are ideal), and small ears, not flying, heavy, or low-set.

The breeder should give you a copy of the dog's pedigree, a Kennel Club registration card and transfer form, or perhaps instead of these a signed registration form, so that you can then register your own puppy.

Every good breeder should also give each puppy purchaser a diet sheet, stating clearly what the puppy is eating at the time of purchase, and the necessary gradual increases in amounts of food and decreases in the number of meals, until adulthood.

Also clearly stated on the sheet should be the dates of worming and the product used, with instructions about future worming—which is necessary for the dog's health and also for the hygiene and health of your own family, especially if you have children. Most important, too, are instructions about the inoculations which can be done, depending upon your veterinary surgeon and the serum that he uses, from the age of eight to twelve weeks. These ward off diseases which could be killers: Distemper/ Hardpad; Virus Hepatitis; Leptospira Canicola; Icterohaemorrhagiae. Two injections are required, a fortnight apart, to give full immunity for one year. (And until the inoculations are completed, don't encourage canine visitors.) Exactly one year after the original two injections it is essential to have a booster injection against all the diseases. Unfortunately this still doesn't give your dog a lifetime of immunity; the Leptospira Canicola and the Icterohaemorrhagiae require an annual booster; this is important whether you live in town or country, as rats and lamp-posts are both sources of infection for these two dangerous diseases. It is also advisable to have a Distemper/Hardpad injection to boost the dog's immunity every three to four years after the first two (done at puppyhood and a year later).

No breeder should sell a Labrador puppy until it has been wormed twice for roundworms. It is a good idea to do a roundworm worming annually, or more often if necessary.

A lot of people have asked me, 'What about these new crippling diseases?' Let me say at once that what they refer to are not 'diseases' at all, but inherited undesirable faults. There is no complete safeguard, because even when the parents are free from such defects, it is still possible for their progeny to be affected. But if you go to a *bona fide* breeder he (or she) will obviously wish to breed sound stock that will be a credit to the kennel name.

I will just mention briefly the faults mostly encountered: Entropion, Hip Dysplasia, Progressive Retinal Atrophy (PRA) and Monorchidism or Cryptorchidism (undescended testicles).

Entropion is the inturning of the bottom eyelid so that the hairs touch the eyeball, setting up a severe irritation which if left untreated can eventually cause blindness. An operation can be done at about five months and should be an effective cure, provided it is carefully and skilfully done. Until the puppy is old enough for the operation, ointments can be supplied by the vet to lessen the irritation.

In *Hip Dysplasia* a 'click' may be heard as the animal sits; obvious signs of discomfort will also be manifest, or there could be a pronounced limp in one of the back legs. Many Labradors have varying degrees of this trouble, but it it not yet known if it is a dominant or recessive fault. Those which do not have a marked degree of hip dysplasia often form compensating muscle, and are indeed able to make useful gundogs and companions, though in old age they may become 'rheumatic'. In some cases surgery has been done to alleviate the condition.

Progressive Retinal Atrophy is a different matter altogether, because a blind dog is no use to anyone, nor

can it enjoy life. In Labradors the blindness is often not noticed unless the dog is in strange surroundings, particularly in twilight or in a dimly lit room, when it may blunder into solid objects; while shooting one might notice that a dog is slow in retrieving what looks like being a simple runner. Usually this defect can appear at three to six years of age, but it can be detected before this by an opthalmic expert. There is a panel of veterinary surgeons approved by the Kennel Club who issue BVA Certificates; an interim certificate can be given from eighteen months onwards, and a permanent one at three years and onwards. So it is a wise precaution to buy a puppy from parents who have these certificates.

Monorchidism and Cryptorchidism: If only one testicle is descended into the scrotum, a dog is often referred to as a 'monorchid'; cryptorchidism exists when both testicles have failed to descend. In technical terms, the former dog is a 'unilateral cryptorchid' and the latter a 'bilateral cryptorchid'. Whereas a monorchid can sire puppies, a true cryptorchid with no testicles descended cannot—though dogs with this fault are often keen to mate, and can indeed be an embarrassment and a nuisance if kept as pets, because they will often try to mate small children or even cushions.

Feeding and Routine
If it is possible, book your chosen puppy in advance and make a firm date and time to go back and collect, so that he will not be fed for at least two hours before the journey—this will help to prevent car sickness. Try to take with you someone to nurse the puppy, holding it firmly on the knees, on a bath towel, and have handy a packet of 'man-sized' paper tissues, just in case. Normally Labradors as a breed are not prone to car sickness. Don't stop en route and let the puppy out, because if it is not yet inoculated there is real danger. On arriving home, put him in the garden so that he has a chance to puddle or perform, then take him inside, and show him his sleeping place (see page 20) and where you intend to keep his water bowl. By now the puppy will probably feel hungry, so offer it a meal.

Your puppy of seven or eight weeks old must have four meals daily, spaced at four-hourly intervals. There should be two milk meals, at breakfast and teatime (warm milk, sweetened with honey or glucose and reinforced with rusks or cereal; alternatively, a puppy milk food may be given). For lunch, soak 'puppy-size' biscuit meal, plus added cod liver oil and seaweed powder, with either tinned meat or cooked beef, cooked heart or cooked paunch, or with one of the proprietary brands of frozen dog food. The supper meal is minced raw beef.

After a week or so, and up to twelve weeks, give $\frac{1}{2}$ pint of milk at tea and again at breakfast, with about 4 heaped tablespoonfuls of soaked biscuit meal (leave it for 20 minutes after soaking in hot stock, to swell and cool) and 4 ounces of cooked meat or tinned meat, together with the vitamins already mentioned. Calcium can be added to milk meals; hard biscuits can be given after the milk meals; and finally, yeast tablets can be given with a small amount of biscuits at bedtime.

Gradually increase the quantities until at four months of age the tea meal is cut out altogether, and at six months

breakfast is no longer given. At this age give at lunch time a soaked biscuit meal with added vitamins and cooked meat (about 8 ounces of meat to 8 heaped tablespoonfuls of soaked meal); at night give 12 ounces of raw meat; yeast tablets can still be given at night, with a handful of biscuits.

At twelve to eighteen months of age—depending upon the size and rate of growth—one meal daily can be given. Vary the diet so that the dog does not become bored. A typical meal would be soaked biscuit meal with cooked heart or paunch, other cooked fresh or frozen meats or tinned meats, plus cod liver oil and seaweed powder; alternatively, give 1 pound of raw beef (it should not be all lean meat, as a proportion of fat is good) without meal or vitamins. Steamed unsmoked fillet of fish can be fed to an off-colour dog. Continue with the vitamin tablets at night, with biscuits.

A heavily used stud dog or a brood bitch, in whelp or feeding a litter, will require a slightly different diet, with bigger quantities. Bone and substance are made from the beginning of pregnancy, and while a brood bitch should not be fed up from the day of mating like cattle for a fatstock show, she does require additional vitamins, and later on more protein and less carbohydrates (see the chapter on Breeding). Labradors have a tendency in middle age to run too fat. Try to prevent this before it happens. Carbohydrates can be cut down and in drastic cases you can obtain a specially made tinned diet, but before using this get the vet's approval. Spaying your Labrador bitch can hasten the onset of obesity, but if the diet and exercise are adjusted accordingly, then this tendency should be kept under control.

Do remember that puppies require just as much rest and sleeping time as a baby, and that routine is very important in helping them become house-trained (see Training chapter).

Make sure your puppy has a suitable place in the house which he can really call his own. A corner in the kitchen away from the doors and cooker is best. At first give him a bed made of a large, stout cardboard box with one side cut

low, and put in it either a piece of old blanket or several layers of newspaper. Whatever you use will get chewed up, so I'd go for newspaper, and it's more hygienic, too. Good alternatives for the adult dog are woodwool—this is the best—or wheat straw. Never use hay—it's too dusty— while barley straw irritates the skin.

If you intend later on to keep your Labrador outside, make sure that his sleeping quarters are warm and free from draughts and damp. His run must be at least six by twelve feet and easy to clean out. It should have fencing at least six feet high; for a bitch I should want it enclosed at the top, so that when she was in season no dog could jump in nor she get out.

Encourage the puppy to go to its bed for a rest or sleep, and see that your children understand that when in his bed the puppy must always be left in peace. The most difficult thing for youngsters to realise about their new puppy is that he is not a clockwork toy and cannot be on the go all the time. And even long-suffering Labradors sometimes feel the need to get away from over-exuberant children.

The first few nights he is with you the puppy will obviously miss his brothers and sisters and may cry a little. Try to bed him down half an hour before you yourself retire so that you can spend a few minutes reassuring him that he isn't going to be left forever and that you are still in the house. Give him a hard biscuit to occupy him when you do finally go, and then *leave* him. Of course he'll cry, and possibly also scratch at the door, but if you go back to him, even to scold him, he will have achieved his object, and will know how to get your company whenever he wants it. (Incidentally, it might be prudent to mention to any close neighbours that there is a new puppy in the house and ask their indulgence should their sleep be disturbed.)

Exercise and Grooming
Until he is about five months old the puppy will get all the exercise he needs playing at home in the garden, and except for a few minutes a day of lead practice (learning to walk to heel, etc.) he should be allowed to decide for himself how much exercise he wants. From five months onwards real exercising can gradually be built up, starting with short walks on the lead, until by the time he is adult he will be getting at least two, preferably three miles a day, or one hour's free running in parks and fields.

After the puppy has settled down—say a week after its arrival—is the time to put on a light rolled leather collar, and also to use a washable nylon lead of serviceable weight. A slip chain might be necessary if you have a very boisterous puppy, but don't get one with fine, small links, because this will hurt the puppy when it pulls tight. Never be tempted, now or later, to buy a harness; these are not safe for a big, strong dog (unless they are made on the lines of an Arctic husky's gear), and they spoil the shoulders; apart from this, they give little or no control to the handler. (See the chapter on Training for method of getting a puppy to go on the lead.)

While the very early months should be comparatively carefree, it's no use leaving your Labrador puppy to run amuck, then suddenly expecting him to learn everything all at once. A little training each day in simple obedience can be given in house or garden, and a surprising amount can be achieved in this way. See the next chapter for details.

The care of the coat is simple—no stripping or trimming is required, and if there is a clean river which is

safe to use, this provides an easy method of keeping the animal free of a doggie smell, for all Labradors adore swimming.

For the actual grooming you need a metal comb with both big and smaller teeth, and a good brush, if possible of nylon and bristle combined. Brush twice weekly, or more often if you wish. A bitch will moult twice a year, about three months after she has been in season. A dog will probably have one big moult a year, with perhaps a second smaller one in either spring or autumn.

Examine the toe nails regularly, to make sure that they are not growing too long—the typical Labrador should have tight 'cat' feet with short nails. If the dew claws are left on, these too will require clipping back so that they do not curve round and grow back into the leg. This can be done with guillotine-type cutters, and is easier when the feet are wet after a walk in grass, because the nails will then be softer. Make sure you don't nick the pink quick, which will be extremely painful and probably put the dog off co-operating ever again. Just remove the tips of the nails, which usually grow longer on the front legs.

Health
Should your puppy seem off-colour at any time, don't hesitate to call the vet. Any persistent vomiting or diarrhoea, particularly if the discharge is blood-stained, must be professionally treated, otherwise in severe cases of enteritis the dog can quickly become dehydrated, causing brain damage and death.

If the puppy or dog swallows a foreign object, this again requires professional treatment. A knob of washing soda, if given soon enough, might cause the dog to vomit the object up. However, if it is a sharp-edged stone or something similar, don't attempt this.

Any heavy discharge from the eyes or nose, or signs of skin trouble, must also be shown to a vet.

It is best to let a bitch have her first season, which can occur at any time between six and eleven months, and then, if it is your intention, have her spayed.

Bad temperament is as a rule the result either of its

being bred into the strain, or of unkindness, ignorance and mishandling. If despite good breeding and treatment you find yourself with a Labrador of uncertain temperament, I do beg of you to tell the breeder and ask for his opinion and aid. There is usually only one final solution—to put down the 'rogue'—and this may be much the kindest and safest thing to do in the end.

ANN WYNYARD
For a number of years Mrs Wynyard has contributed to the Labrador Breed Note Column of the *Dog World* weekly paper, so I put yet another feather in my cap when she agreed to write the chapter on this breed as a pet. She was given her first Labrador in 1939, at the outbreak of the last war, to prevent it from being destroyed. After the war and from this almost accidental beginning, the Wynyards established the small, select Braedale Kennels. There they bred working Labradors that have in the past been in great demand by shooting men and women in Oxfordshire, Buckinghamshire and Northamptonshire. Getting the dog show bug, Mrs Wynyard realised that although her strain had brains, it was not exactly up to championship standard when it came to the beauty stakes. Come 1956, and the kennels bought in a bitch by the name of Diant Joy who played a great part in the process of making the kennel's strain dual-purpose. Not just pretty faces, but dogs that were intelligent *and* handsome— surely ideal pets. (Which is what the books in this series are all about.) The 'Braeduke' Labradors have produced winners in the show ring, as well as in field trials in Britain, Canada, India, Singapore and Australia, and Mrs Wynyard has judged the breed not only in the British Isles but also in Holland, South Africa and Rhodesia.

J.C.

2 Living with your Labrador

BY JO COULSON

Later in this book you will find an excellent chapter on general training, but here I am giving you ideas gleaned from my experience with this particular breed. Labradors are very intelligent dogs and will use their brains either for or against their owners. While an unruly, untrained dog is a menace to the community, well-trained Labradors can be, and are, used in many different ways. Few things give greater pleasure than the sight of a man and his dog working together as a team—think for example of an expert guide dog or gundog. You can establish the same working relationship with your pet Labrador. From the first day you have him, he must be made to realise that you, his owner, are the undisputed boss and that what you say goes. I know from personal experience how easy it is to give way and make allowances for a sweet cuddly puppy, but even an eight-week-old pup can sense your hesitation or lack of authority and will soon learn how to wheedle his way out of doing something he doesn't want to do.

The first lessons in obedience can start as soon as you get the new puppy home. The way to a Labrador's brain is through his stomach, and a few moments of basic training around meal-times will soon begin to have the desired effect. (See 'Learning Commands', below.) As long as you have his dish of food in sight you'll have his undivided attention—but do keep the lessons short, or he'll drown you, for Labradors are great dribblers. And talking of food and training, I strongly advise that from the outset you make a firm rule that the dog is fed only at his proper meal-times and that he should not be given odd tit-bits. All through their lives Labradors try to con the world that they are half-starved. The consequence is that thousands of Labradors are walking, or rather tottering, around with a vast middle-age spread. Start as you mean to go on, and your dog will be healthier and live longer. Get your children to co-operate in this; explain that just as they don't expect to eat bits from the dog's plate, so the dog is not entitled to morsels from theirs. Because of this greed, the Labrador must be taught not to stand up on his hind

legs to examine the contents of the kitchen or dining table. A rolled-up newspaper slapped against the legs is a good deterrent.

Another point, while on the subject of food, is the sad fact that Labradors are frightful chewers. Your shoes, the chair legs, the carpet, anything they can get their teeth into. The problem is that, like young babies, when they are teething they really need something to gnaw on, and between the ages of about five and nine months Labradors are in the process of cutting those enormous back teeth, so they simply have to chew. Bearing this in mind, try to

keep your puppy supplied with raw beef marrow bones—but make sure that the butcher saws the bones and doesn't chop them, as splinters of bone can be very dangerous internally. Provide also suitable-sized 'beef chews'—these can be eaten on the most priceless carpets, because they are not at all messy, nor are they indigestible if swallowed.

Teach your puppy from the start to let you take his bone or chew away from him, talking softly and praising him while you do so. Then give it back, to show there is no evil intent. He will gradually learn. You don't want a dog with an overpowering guarding instinct, who won't let you touch him when he is eating or playing with his toys or bones.

During the early days at least you'll have to make sure that things you don't want the dog to chew are not within his reach. Particularly, make sure that all electric flexes are either removed or, if this is not possible, replaced by special heavy-duty cable. I own a dog who has on three occasions bitten clean through electric wiring carrying enough volts to kill him, and since I can't pass on the secret of his lucky escapes, I can only warn you. Make sure too that all plastic articles are out of reach, because this substance could cause an internal blockage if swallowed, and it doesn't show up on an X-ray. For the same reason I don't advocate giving Labradors small

rubber balls—buy them plenty big enough, and be sure they are of the special reinforced rubber type made for dogs.

Because they have such strong retrieving instincts, all Labradors enjoy carrying things, whether they have been gun-trained or not. How often have you seen a Labrador, born and bred in a city, proudly carrying his owner's newspaper or small parcel down the High Street, or been greeted at the door of a friend's house by a tail-wagging Labrador with a shoe in its mouth? It is advisable, however, to keep an eye on just *what* is being transported with such loving care. I have been caught out before now by a mischievous-looking dog carrying some small unidentifiable object and, having let my curiosity get the better of me, been presented with a long-dead mouse. And even the most sensible dogs occasionally do something stupid like carrying a milk bottle from the kitchen. In our house slippers have a habit of disappearing, only to be found days later, rain-sodden and unwearable, in a far corner of the garden. However, if you wish to encourage the retrieving instinct for future use, it's no good calling your 'naughty' puppy to you and then smacking him for doing what comes naturally. Better to capitalise on the instinct from the beginning by providing him with one or two of his own toys in safe materials that are solid enough to be carried around. If you have any ambitions to gun-train him, he can be started with an old sock or a nylon stocking cut to the right length and filled with kapok, which floats and doesn't become waterlogged. Weights can gradually be added inside, to accustom the dog to carrying heavier objects.

Learning Commands
Learning to sit by order is an important lesson. A few times a day push gently on the puppy's hindquarters while the word 'sit' is given as a loud, clear command (but don't shout). This can be connected with the signal of a forefinger raised in admonishment. As I said, a good time to teach this is at meal-times, when the second command, 'Wait!' can also be given, to restrain the natural eagerness of the puppy to get to his food bowl. To 'break' this command make a sweeping movement of the arm, point to the food bowl and command 'Fetch', or say 'Good dog!'

The next step is again to press the haunches (gently, because damage can be done to the hindquarters by too strong pressure) and to make the puppy sit in one spot. Hold up the finger and slowly walk away—backwards at first, so that you can return to the puppy and again push down the haunches with the command 'Sit!' or 'Stay!' Don't lose your temper if the puppy—naturally at first— moves forward towards you as you move away. This exercise will take a lot of practice, and can be kept up even when the dog is adult.

Teaching the puppy to walk to heel on the lead can be done by passing the lead behind your body and holding it in your right hand while the puppy is made to walk on your left-hand side. Use a long lead, so that you can gradually tighten and shorten it to bring the puppy back to the required pace. (Later on, when doing this exercise off the lead, a rolled-up newspaper can be gently tapped on the dog's nose if it intrudes too far past your left knee.) The word 'Heel!' should be given, with a sharp pull on the lead to prevent the dog straining forward. This is a most important part of the training. After all, an adult Labrador bitch (at eighteen months and over) should when

in show condition weigh about sixty pounds, though less when in good hard working condition at the end of a shooting season; a male will weigh more. So you must be able to keep these strong and often boisterous animals under control. Nothing is worse than the sight of a harassed woman with a pram, both being towed along at a rate of knots by an undisciplined dog.

It is neither wise nor clever to encourage a Labrador to chase cats—especially if you have any ambition to do a little shooting (however rough) at any time in the future. A big dog out of control in the shooting field is just as much of a disgrace as a dog out of control on a public highway or in a field with cattle or sheep.

Labradors don't really make guard dogs—they are only too eager to welcome and make friends with anyone who knocks at your door. But they do give vocal warning of anyone approaching the house, and this is usually enough to deter most unwelcome visitors. However, I believe that while your dog should not be stopped from barking when he has cause, he should learn that needless, prolonged barking is anti-social and not allowed. Similarly, he should learn that while it is polite to show pleasure when visitors arrive, jumping up is forbidden.

Kennelling
Early in your young dog's life should come the training for something that I consider to be one of the hardest lessons to be learned with a Labrador. That is the ability to kennel your dog when necessary. The discipline involves the owner, not the dog, for believe me, dogs do not dislike going into good kennels. True, they will try to make you *think* they hate it; they will back away from the proprietor, shy away from the kennel, and bark at you as you walk away, but the moment you've gone out of sight your dog will start looking around him, sniffing the new smells and deciding how much sympathy he can wring out of the kennel maid. It took me years to realise that my beloved dogs would not pine to death if I left them for a few days—consequently I was their slave, and fast becoming neurotic as well.

Obviously, you will choose kennels you feel are well-run and will suit your dog. Some time before the proposed visit, ask to look over various local boarding kennels. Most reputable establishments are quite happy to show prospective clients their facilities, usually by appointment, and personally I wouldn't consider letting my dogs go to a kennel I had not first seen. Often one can select a place as a result of personal recommendation, which is surely the best method.

Then I would advise a trial run. While your dog is still young (between nine and twelve months) arrange to put him into kennels for just a day or two, perhaps a weekend, so that he will learn at an early stage that from time to time he will be going to this strange and exciting place; after his first short stay he will be secure in the knowledge that you will be coming back for him. So long as you have left with the kennels an address at which you can be contacted if need be, you can go off on your holidays without any worries. You will certainly be assured of a rapturous welcome home!

Summing Up

If in the formative stage of his life you have taught your Labrador the way you expect him to conduct himself, you will by the time he is about eighteen months old have quite the most delightful companion imaginable. He will respond to your moods, be sad with you or glad with you as the occasion demands. Labradors are the comedians of the canine world and their greatest pleasure is in keeping their audience amused. The supply of new tricks is endless, and if you once react favourably to some little thing your pet does, he'll never forget it and will make that his party piece for years to come. I'm bound to admit that Labradors never really grow up, and even an eight- or nine-year-old will still behave like a six-month-old puppy just when you least expect it.

Don't misunderstand me, though: life with a Labrador is not quite so nerve-shattering as I have perhaps made it sound. It's just that every sixty-five-pound package of bones and fur has such a non-stop supply of energy and *joie de*

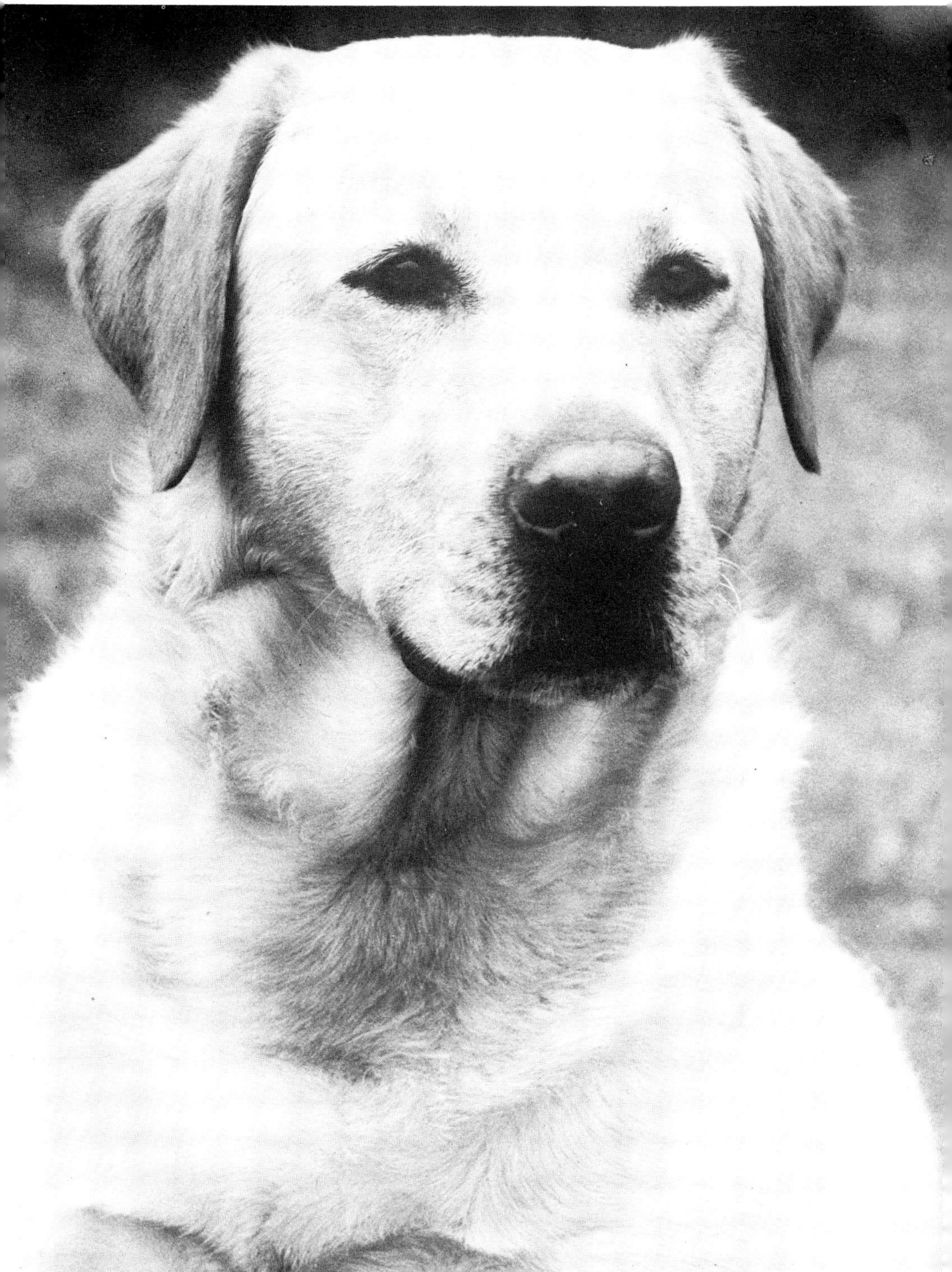

vivre that there simply is never a dull moment.

There are, however, occasional glimmers of hope, when even a rip-roaring monster will realise that he is required to put on his party manners, so that Great-Aunt Maude, on her annual visit, will see not the prize fool of the year, but a sweet obedient dog who sits quietly at her feet wearing a 'butter-wouldn't-melt-in-the-mouth' expression.

An expert con man, a brilliant comedy actor, and quite the most delightful companion ever—that's the Labrador.

JO COULSON
Mrs Jo Coulson came from a family that bred Alsatians, Cocker Spaniels and the occasional Collie. After her marriage, she settled for the Labrador as a pet. At present the Coulson family has no fewer than seven—all house pets. Though Jo Coulson is now a Labrador breeder and exhibitor to be reckoned with, and a show judge rapidly making her mark with gundogs, I feel that to

her Labradors will first and foremost always be pets. It was in 1964 that Jo bought her first Labrador, and almost at once started to do the rounds of the small local dog shows. Flushed with success at this level, she was truly bitten by the show dog bug, and gradually turned her interest to open and championship show competitions. At the same time she increased her kennel to the present number. In 1970 she bred her first litter, and it was with one of these dogs that Mrs Coulson won Best of Breed at the 1972 Crufts Show at Olympia. This home-bred Labrador also had the honour of being a finalist in the Gundog Group at the same show—a great achievement in any breed, and most certainly in such a powerful and highly competitive breed as the Labrador Retriever.

J.C.

3 History of the Labrador Retriever
BY MICHAEL BOOTHROYD

The Labrador is now freely acknowledged to be the most popular of all the Retriever varieties (the others being Curly-coated, Flat-coated and Golden Retriever) and has for some time topped the gundog registrations at the Kennel Club.

Labradors were originally found not in Labrador, but in Newfoundland, where they were used by the people who lived on the wild and rugged coastline. This distinctive black water dog was developed for general utility purposes, and in particular was expected to retrieve the fish that slipped out of the nets on the surface of the icy sea and to carry rope ends and messages from ship to shore. With their short but dense coat Labradors were well adapted to cope with the freezing snow and bitter Arctic winds. They were very active, fast both on land and in the water, and well able to look after themselves, being noted for their prowess in fighting.

There are several ideas about their first appearance in Britain. It is said that some of the smaller smooth-coated black 'Newfoundlands', sometimes called the 'St. John's Newfoundlands', made their way over to England in the 1820's by way of the cod boats which came into Poole Harbour. These dogs came into the hands of a few shooting men who found that their retrieving, their noses and their excellent water work made them invaluable. With a few exceptions, however, the breed was virtually lost or absorbed into other English shooting dog strains. It was not until the 1870's and 80's that the Duke of Buccleugh, the Earl of Home and one or two other well-known shooting men bred dogs from a few new importations and from the rather mixed blood left over from the earlier importations to Poole Harbour. Thus the breed emerged as the 'Labrador', in the same type and form as had been seen in Newfoundland. This same type persists to the present day.

Labradors soon became very popular, especially with gamekeepers and sportsmen. They have for many years been included in the Royal kennels at Sandringham, and it will be remembered that the Queen and Princess Anne both visited the Labrador ring on their visits to Crufts.

Most of the early Labradors were black, the yellows appearing around 1900. The yellows were at first looked down on, and although they gradually became popular, it was not until after the First World War that they began to be considered as show dogs. Earlier on, many yellow dogs had unfortunately been drowned at birth. Mrs Veronica Wormald of the well-known 'Knaith' prefix pioneered the yellow colour, and eventually had a very strong kennel of famous yellow champions, such as Ch. Knaith Banjo, a dual champion.

Other celebrated foundation kennels were those of the Buccleughs, the Mundens and, of course, Lorna, Countess Howe's 'Banchory' strain, which really dominated the show scene and field trials and must have done more than any other kennel to popularise the breed. In fact, the whole of today's Labrador world owes a great debt of gratitude to the Countess for her loyalty to the breed and for her keen interest in the working side. Behind her famous kennel stands that great sire, Dual Ch. Banchory Bolo, a black dog, ancestor to many of today's outstanding champions.

During the early years many famous kennels were started, particularly Mr Keith Hart's Landyke kennels at Knipton Grantham, which has a very strong team of yellows, now housing such well-known dogs as Ch. Landyke Velour, Ch. Landyke Stormer and Ch. Landyke Lancer (litter brothers). Ch. Landyke Teal was the last to make up into a champion in this country.

Mr Maurice Gilliat, in partnership with his daughter Daphne, made up a few 'Holton' champions; one of these was the famous Ch. Holton Baron, who holds the breed record number of certificates—twenty-five—and was nineteen times best of breed; in addition Baron won fifteen reserve challenge certificates. Mr Gilliat's kennel, which was established long before the last war, is still going strong.

Mr and Mrs Wilson Jones owned the Diant kennels and bred such famous dogs as Ch. Diant Juliet, and also owned Ch. Diant Swandyke Cream Cracker. Mr Fred Wrigley of Rotherham made a great impact on the breed with his many yellow 'Kinley' champions: Ch. Kinley Melody, Ch. Kinley Curlew of Upallthwaite, Ch. Kinley Charm, Ch. Kinley Copper and Ch. Kinley Skipper. Mr Wrigley is one of the most respected and most sought-after judges both here and abroad.

Mr and Mrs Grant Cairns of Glasgow made up many champions under the 'Blaircourt' affix: Ch. Imp of Blaircourt, Ch. Tessa of Blaircourt, Ch. Ruler of Blaircourt. The strain will be mentioned in most Labrador pedigrees through the famous Ch. Sandylands Tweed of Blaircourt, which was purchased at eight weeks by Mrs Gwen Broadley (see below). This dog has probably sired more champions than any other stud dog in the breed.
Mr and Mrs Horace Taylor of Matlock owned that striking black dog, Ch. Watstandwell Dallyduff Robin, who was a most famous sire as well as a great show dog. They also bred Ch. Ballyduff Watstandwell Rowene and Ch. Watstandwell Coronet, and these dogs made a great impact on the breed as a whole. Ch. Watstandwell Ballyduff Robin was the sire of the two sisters, Ch. Romantic of Coohoy and Ch. Roberta of Coohoy, which were bred by

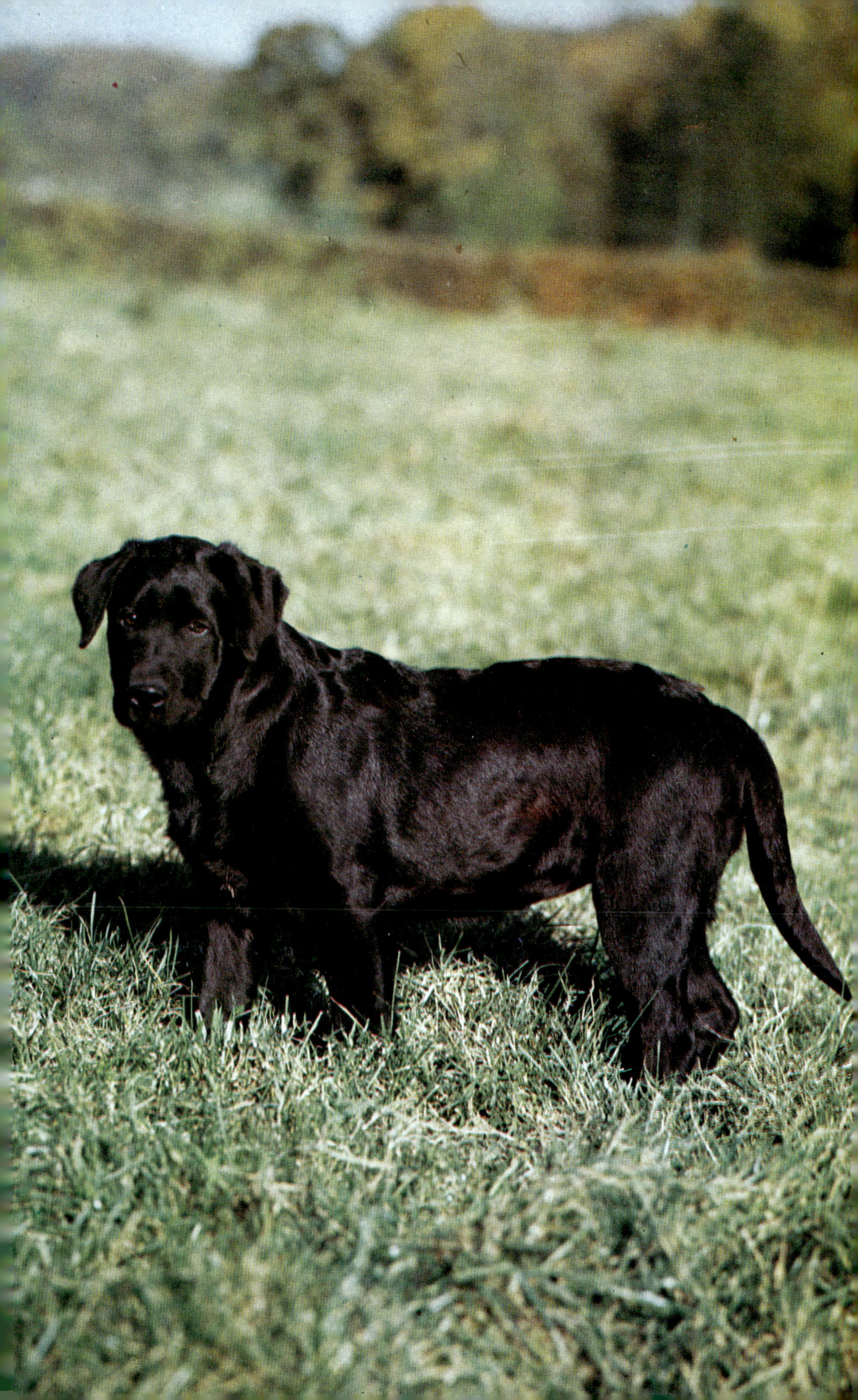

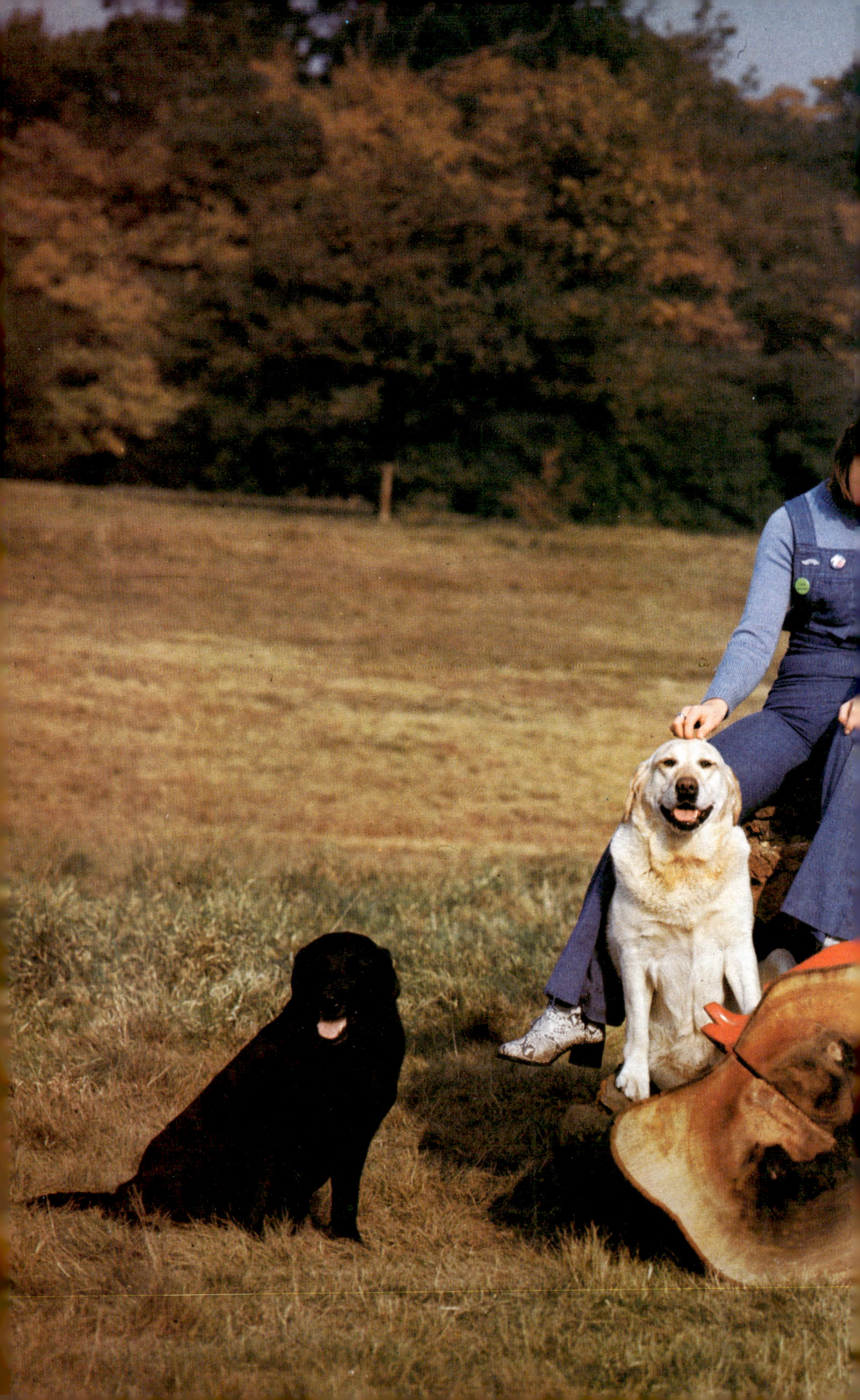

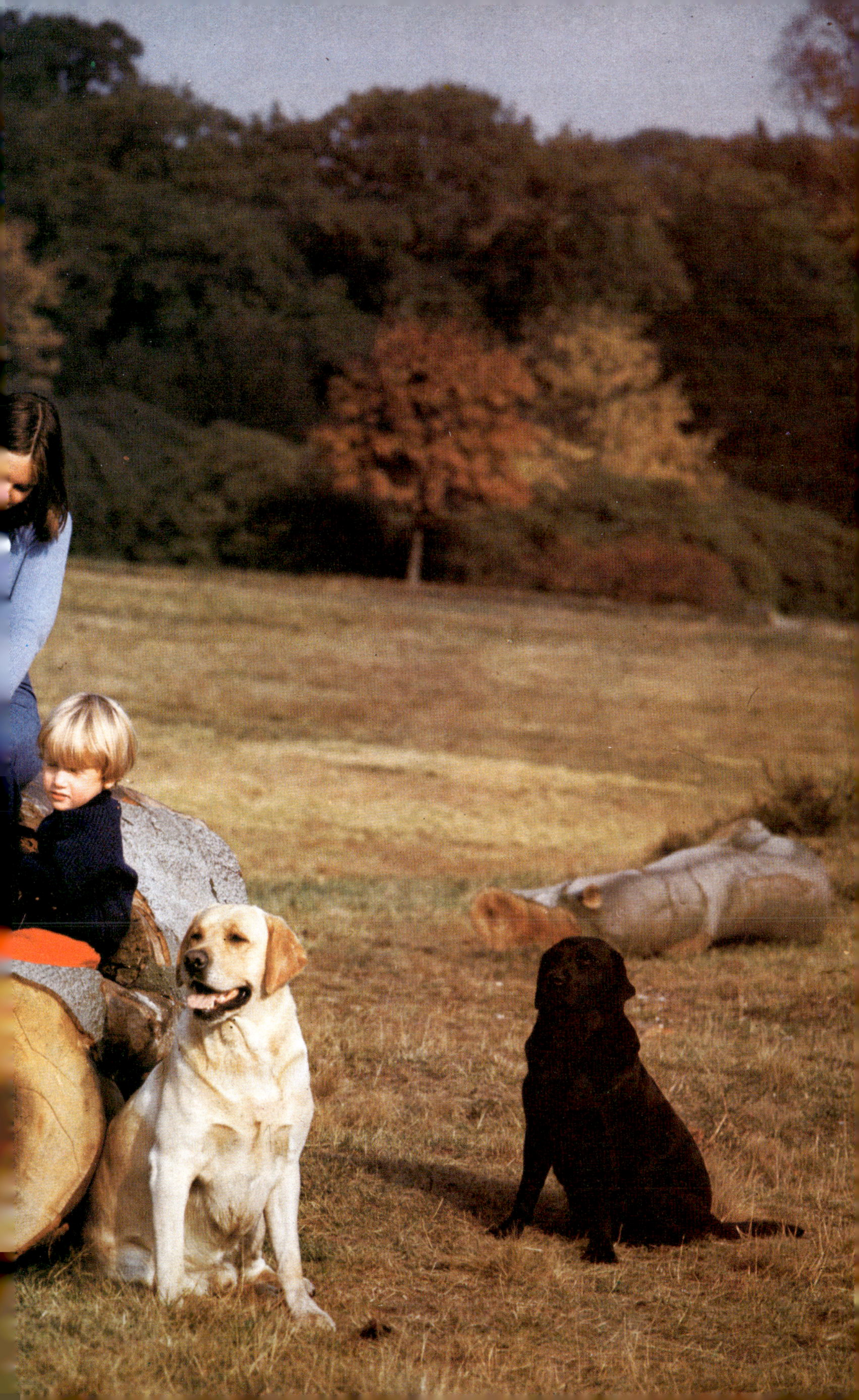

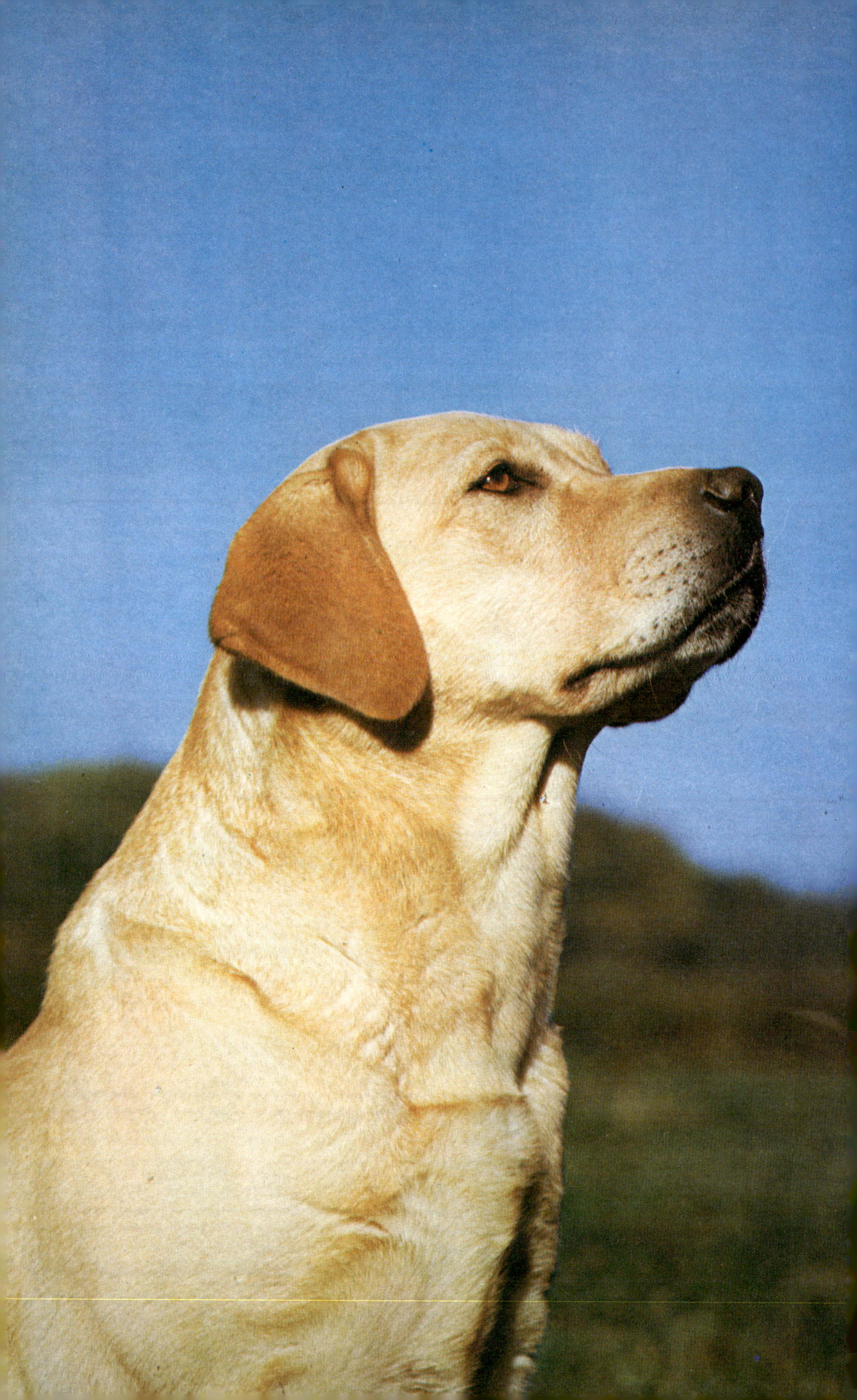

Mrs D. Cliffe of Huddersfield. She had a strong kennel of black bitches, including Coquette of Coohoy (winner of two challenge certificates and eleven reserves), which must go down into history as the most unlucky of animals not to have gained her title.

Mrs Bridget Docking, down in Norfolk, has long been a well-known figure, making up several champions, and was the breeder of Ch. Watstandwell Ballyduff Robin. Her more recent champions include Ch. Ballyduff Hollybranch of Keithray, Ch. Ballyduff Seaman, Ch. Ballyduff Marina, and so on—all these being full champions as well as good sires.

Mrs Peggy Rae of Braintree, Essex, has concentrated on yellows; she made up Ch. Cornlands Westelm Flight and also bred Ch. Cornlands Peter So Gay. Next came Ch. Cornlands Landy, followed by Ch. Cornlands Kimvalley Crofter (bred by Mrs Diana Beckett), which sired Peggy's most famous Labrador bitch, Ch. Cornlands My Fair Lady; she won close on twenty challenge certificates, and shared the double at Crufts in 1968 with Ch. Cornlands Nokeener Highlight. This dog was bred by Mrs R. Williams of Brecon, who produced many winners that have been campaigned by other breeders; Aust. Ch. Pichbeck Nokeener Harvest Home made his mark here before he left, being the sire of the litter sisters Sh. Ch. Sandylands Honour and Sh. Ch. Sandylands Holly. Mrs Williams' own Ch. Nokeener Moon Rocket was made up in 1970 (as I well remember, since I won the bitch CC with my own Sh. Ch. Roydwood Right on Time on two occasions when Moon Rocket won the dog certificates).

Probably today's foremost kennel in the breed, owning many of the leading sires, is the Sandylands establishment situated near Daventry and belonging to Mrs Gwen Broadley, who is one of our most famous judges both here and abroad. I cannot mention all the champions she has made up, but nearly every Labrador pedigree has somewhere in it the black dog Ch. Sandylands Tweed of Blaircourt (mentioned above), which she bought as a puppy. He sired well over twenty champions and show champions. His grandson, the famous Ch. Sandylands

Tandy, a great yellow dog, has sired close on the same number of champions; Sandylands June and Jerry, Trutt, Dancer, Mark, Gary, and My Lad are just a few of the well-known champions bred at these kennels. Mrs Broadley's long experience in the breed and her vast knowledge are available to any novice starting in the breed, and she has put many people on the road to success by selling them good foundation stock.

The Wilkinsons of 'Keithray' Labradors at Bradford started with an unregistered black bitch puppy of the famous 'Cookridge' strain bought from Mrs Pauling at Tadcaster. This puppy was acquired for their son's birthday present. Later she was registered as Hollybank Beauty, and quickly became a full champion, winning her six CCs very quickly. She was mated to Ch. Sandylands Tweed of Blaircourt and in her first litter produced four champions; in her second she produced two bred in the same way, thus starting her owners on the way to fame, both here and abroad. There are many more famous kennels in the north. Margaret Ward has a very well-established one with the 'Heatheredge' prefix, and then there are Mary Roslin Williams with her kennel of 'Mansergh' blacks in Sedbergh and the 'Glenharveys' owned by Mrs J. Harvey of Shipley. Mrs Jean Hurley of Ripponden made up Ch. Standwood Leda and also has a very strong team of both blacks and yellows. I could go on. . . .

MICHAEL BOOTHROYD

Michael John Boothroyd's father and grandfather were both farmers, so he was brought up with an agricultural background. He started breeding Rough Collies at the age of ten, and later went into the showing and breeding of Cocker Spaniels. With much more success he then added English Springers and bred the Danish and Norwegian Ch. Roydwood Russian Sable. Mr Boothroyd handled the yellow Labrador dog Ch. Hollybunch of Keithray and helped him achieve his title—and so began his interest in Labradors. He showed and owned Sh. Ch. Tanya of Keithray, winner of six CCs and Best of Breed at Crufts in 1967. Among notable dogs he has bred are the Italian Ch. Roydwood Reveller, who sired Sh. Ch. Roydwood Right on Time, winner of eight CCs and eight reserve CCs and Group winner; Sh. Ch. Roydwood Royal Tara, winner of three CCs and three Reserve CCs; Roydwood Royal Tan, winner of three Reserve CCs; Arg. Ch. Roydwood Recorder, a Cocker Spaniel who won CCs here before going abroad; Int. Ch. Roydwood Right Reply, winner in Sweden, and many more top winning Cockers. Rottweilers and Shih Tzu's are other breeds he has tried, and examples have been shown with much success at championship shows. The kennel has also housed Pekes and Cavaliers.

Mr Boothroyd judged his first show at the age of seventeen, then awarded CCs in Cockers and in Welsh Corgis, both Pembroke and Cardigan (Corgis being a breed in which he has always taken the greatest interest, though he has never kept any). He has judged English Springers and Labradors, and is now passed to judge Golden Retrievers. At championship shows he has judged King Charles, Pointers and German Pointers. He has judged in Finland, Denmark and Sweden (three times); he has also judged the Danish Retriever championship show twice.

J.C.

4 Training

BY JOHN HOLMES

The first essential in training is not patience or love of animals as so many people think. And it is not a knowledge of how to make a dog sit, lie down, or take up any other position, as some books would have us believe. The first essential is what I call dog sense – a knowledge of canine mentality – giving one the ability to understand what makes a dog tick.

The reason why the dog is so much easier to train than the cat (which has been domesticated for just as long) is not because it is more intelligent. It is because the dog is a pack animal while the cat prefers a more or less solitary existence. In a pack of dogs there is a very highly developed social order with a leader and followers in a very definite order – top dogs and underdogs, so to speak. One also finds top cats and undercats but there is a vast difference. Whereas the underdogs actually obey and follow their leaders, an undercat simply keeps out of the way of a top cat. The dog's natural instinct is, therefore, to obey a leader, while a cat only wants to please itself, which means that a dog can be made to do certain things we want even when he does not like doing them, while a cat can only be persuaded to do things it likes doing.

One of the most remarkable features of the domestic dog is the extent to which it still retains the mental characteristics of its wild ancestry. Man has created a larger variety of canine types than in any other domestic species. It is hard to believe that the Pekingese and the Great Dane, the Chihuahua and the Irish Wolfhound all have the same common ancestry. By looking at them one could be excused for saying 'It's impossible!'. But by studying their mental make-up one becomes more and more aware of the similarity in all breeds. Of course different breeds, produced for different jobs, have certain differences in mentality but they are not nearly as great as is generally believed. It is certainly much less than the different opinions of their breeders. Ask a dedicated breeder of *any* breed and he or she will tell you that it is definitely different from *all* other breeds and of course better in every way. And these people honestly believe what they say for the simple reason that they have never owned any other breed and are so wrapped up in their own that they never even see the breed being judged in the next ring at a dog show. I mention this because I believe that much confusion in training is caused by the idea that each breed has a completely different mentality.

In my time I have trained many dogs for many purposes – film dogs, gun dogs, sheepdogs, guard dogs, working terriers, etc., and I have found that the basic principles of training apply to all dogs of all breeds and indeed to all animals.

The first principle is that by nature the dog wants a leader that it can respect and obey. And he is quite willing, indeed grateful, to be led by a human pack leader. This does not mean that dogs are almost human and it is a dreadful insult to the canine species to suggest that they are. It simply means that we are all animals and many of us are capable of taking on the rôle of pack leader, providing that we are more intelligent and stronger willed than the animal we want to obey us. That many are not is evidenced by the number of disobedient, trouble-making dogs to be seen everywhere.

Here we have a two-way problem. The majority of dogs are what is known as submissive and want to follow a leader but a few are born to be leaders and are known as dominant dogs. Exactly the same happens in the human race and, although we do not usually talk about dominant and submissive people, many readers will know what I mean. The problem usually arises from the fact that a submissive person can rarely train a dominant dog. It is for this reason that a dog will often obey one member of the family and not another. Normally a dog obeys the father first, the mother second and treats young children as equals. But sometimes the dog will obey the mother and take no notice of what the father says. I have invariably found in such cases that the husband obeys the wife too! A dominant person rarely gets the same pleasure from a submissive dog as from a fairly dominant one. Although easy to train to a high standard I get little pleasure from training submissive dogs. All the dogs which stand out in my memory as 'greats' have been dominant, many of them bloody-minded awkward brutes which had been discarded by their previous owners.

This is not a chapter on how to choose a dog but, if you have not already bought one, you should pay particular attention to this point. A person who cannot train one dog may get another *of the same breed* and train it to perfection. Likewise the dog which that person failed to train may go to someone else who will train it quite easily.

The next principle is that dogs do not reason as we do. Here there is considerable difference of opinion. On the one hand there are scientists who say that man is the only animal which reasons. On the other there are people who claim that their dog not only understands every word they say to it but actually talks to them as well, and they carry on regular conversations. Most scientists study dogs under clinical conditions which are quite unnatural. Nothing could be more unnatural than the conditions under which the average domestic dog lives but these are still very different from laboratory conditions, and many pet owners

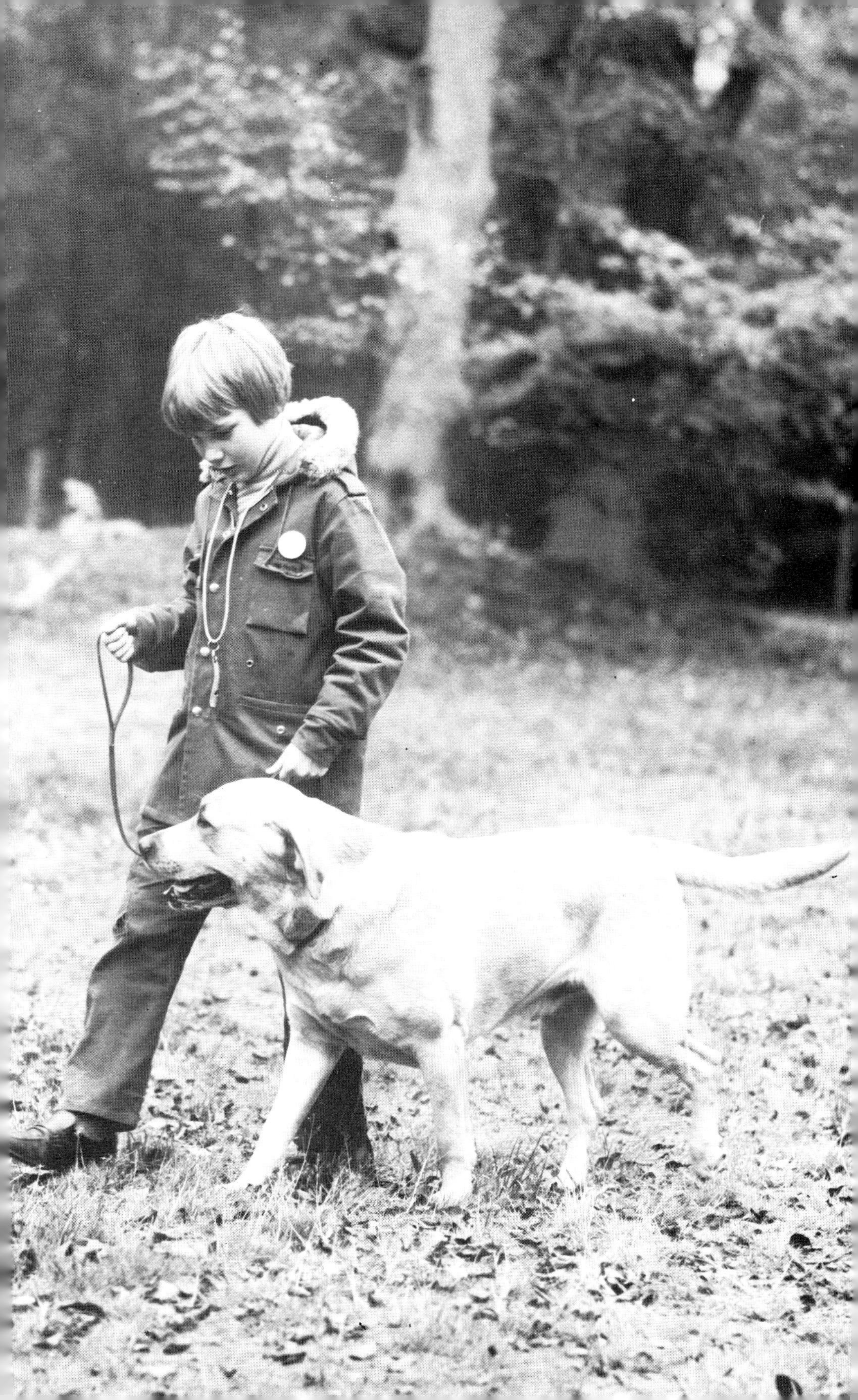

are so preoccupied with turning their dearly beloved into a four-legged human being that they really do believe it does many of the stupid things people do and they never allow it to do any of the clever things which dogs can do.

In my opinion dogs do sometimes reason to a considerable extent. But we cannot really say to what extent and, as the dog cannot tell us, it is unlikely that we shall ever know. What trainers have learned from experience is that to attempt to train an animal is doomed to failure if it is assumed that it can reason. All training must, therefore, be based on the assumption that *dogs do not reason*.

Dogs learn by association of ideas. They associate certain sounds or sights with pleasure or displeasure. They tend to do the things naturally which result in pleasure and refrain from those which create displeasure. I believe that a dog associates sounds and sights in exactly the same way as we do. All of us can think of a tune, the sound of waves breaking on the seashore, gunfire, a police car siren or one of many other sounds which bring back vivid memories – pleasant or unpleasant – every time we hear them. Likewise with things we have seen and the same sight and sound may well bring back either pleasant or unpleasant memories, like the sight of a telegram messenger who may bring either good or bad news. The most important thing to remember is that the more pleasant or unpleasant the experience the stronger the association of ideas. To most of us a telegram does not do very much but those who have received tragic news by telegram become apprehensive, even terrified, of opening another one. In the same way, those who have received glad tidings by telegram will not be apprehensive of receiving one in the future, knowing quite well that it may not bring good news.

The strongest association is built up by fear. If a child gets bitten by a dog it will be excused for having a lifetime fear of dogs. But if a puppy gets kicked by a child people will wonder why it develops a lifelong fear of children and the breeder will be accused of selling a dog with a bad temperament.

First associations are usually much stronger than subsequent ones. If a child has a very unpleasant experience

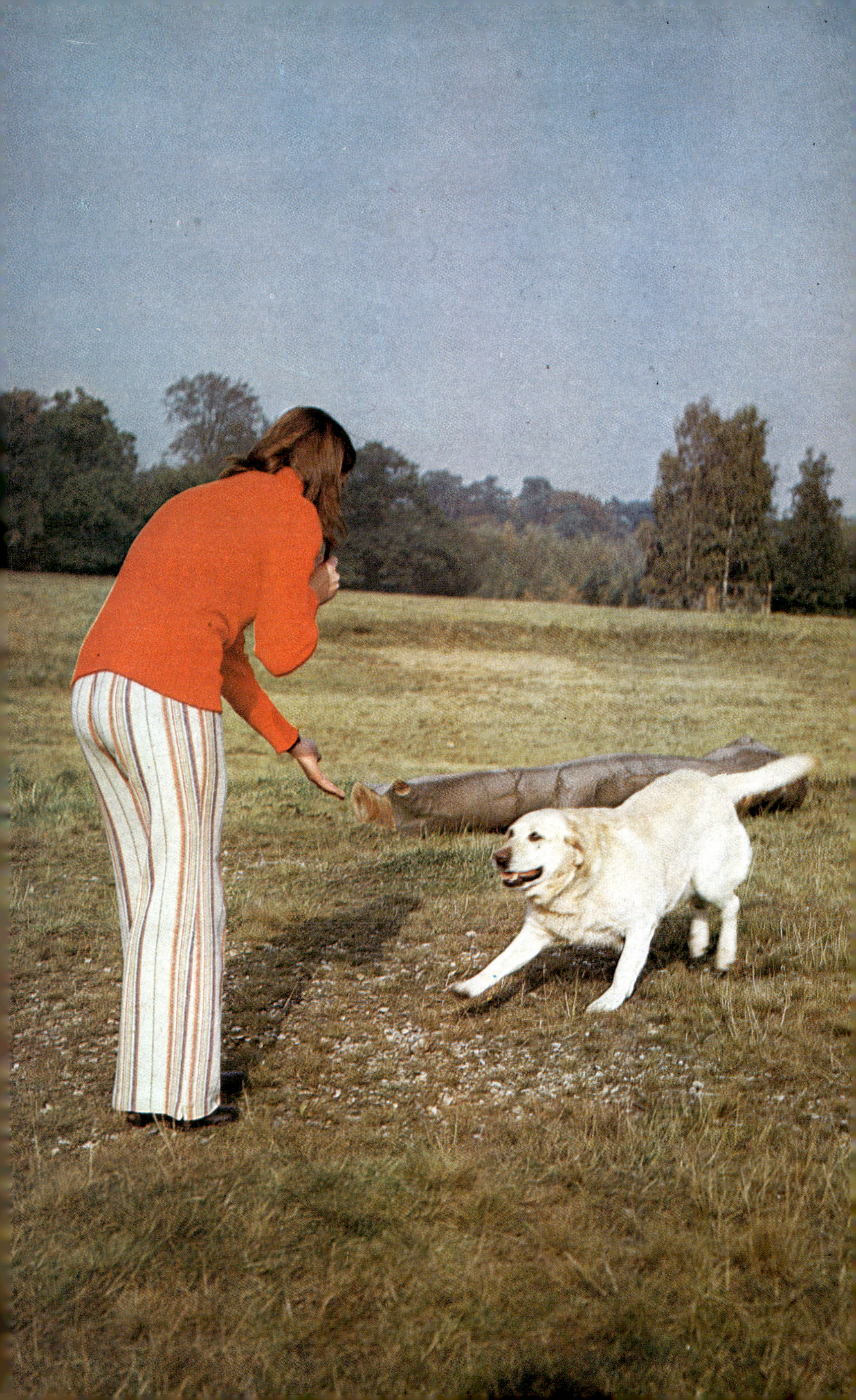

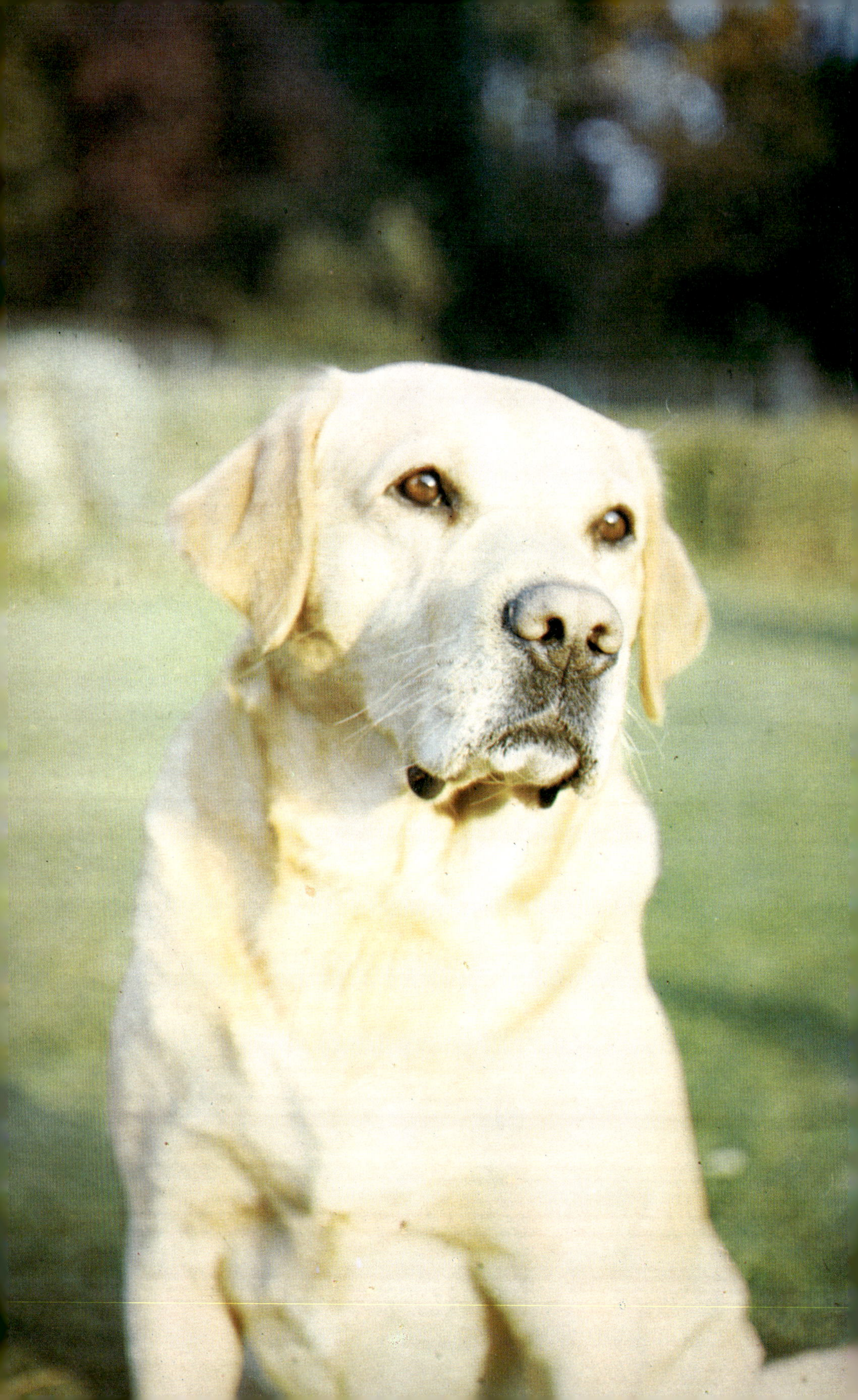

on the first day at school he or she may take a long time to get over it. If this had not occurred until several weeks at school had passed, it might have had little or no effect. People who show dogs know that if a puppy gets a bad fright at its first show it may dislike shows for life. The same experience a year later might have no effect at all.

Another point worth remembering is that dogs, like us, are much more easily upset and with much more lasting effect when they are off colour. An experience which would have little or no effect under normal circumstances can have disastrous results if it happens when a puppy is teething or has a virus infection, or when a bitch is in season, especially for the first time, and in many cases the animal shows no real symptoms of illness.

For training purposes we try to create the association of ideas which we want in the dog and we do it by correction and reward. This means that we try to make it unpleasant for the dog to do the things we don't want him to do and pleasant for him to do the things we do want. The best example of how we should do this is to be seen by studying a bitch with puppies. First of all she supplies them with food from her own mammary glands and later partly digested food which she regurgitates for them. She also licks and caresses them and makes friendly soft noises which fall somewhere between grunting and whining. The puppies, therefore, associate her with food and caressing and every time they see, hear or smell her they rush joyously to her, just as everyone hopes their new puppy will rush to them; if they feed it, fondle and pet it and make friendly noises to it the chances are that this will happen.

Most people in fact do this, overlooking the fact that the bitch's training does not end there. As the puppies become bigger the bitch, without losing interest in them, does not want to be mauled about by them all the time. Many dog owners put up with that but bitches usually have more sense! So, when the puppies become a bit overbearing the bitch growls at them. Many pups react instinctively to a growl and will stop what they are doing, be it chewing the mother's ear or tail or trying to suckle when there is no milk at the bar, but some bold, dominant pups pay little or no attention. The bitch then repeats her threat and, if there is no response, she will snap at the puppy, often hurting it quite badly human standards. But she does not hurt it often. Next time the puppy hears an angry growl it associates it with a snap and quickly responds. If it does not, it gets another and another until it *does* respond. When a bitch snaps at a puppy it usually gets a fright and runs away a little distance. But it soon crawls back to be licked and caressed and will soon be happy again.

    From this I hope you will realise that far from being unnatural, as some people would have use believe, training is the most natural thing in the world, and the bitch with her puppies (many other animals are similar) is an excellent example of simple and straightforward association of ideas. Once upon a time dogs and children were trained according to these simple principles. We have now become more highly educated and use big words like psychiatrist and psychoanalysis – we even have canine psychologists who have never kept a dog in their lives – and everywhere we find disobedient and unhappy dogs and children.

The dog has a simple straightforward mind. He is highly intelligent but less intelligent than we are. If you are less intelligent than your dog just forget about trying to train him! Most of his senses and instincts are far stronger than ours. He sees as well as we do but, because he is nearer the ground and cannot see what we see, many people say his sight is inferior. He hears many times better than we do but from the shouting at many training classes one could believe that all dogs were deaf. His memory is as good if not better than ours, yet people will marvel at their dog recognising them after a six-week holiday. It would be just as logical to be unable to recognise one's own family – and the dog – after that period. Bearing all the above facts in mind let us now try to apply them to the new puppy you have just bought.

To start with remember that he is only a baby suddenly removed from his mother and probably his brothers and sisters too. At this stage he does not want a leader as much as a comforter to replace his mother. Generally speaking women are much better than men at giving confidence to young animals and it is fortunate that in most households it is the woman who takes the new puppy under her wing. This is not just an idea of my own. The Guide Dogs for the Blind Association employs girls to look after the puppies and to do the initial training while men take over the more advanced training when the dog is old enough to need a leader.

You may have noticed when I was talking about creating associations of ideas I said that we *try* to create those we want and avoid those we do not want. But many wrong associations are built up by ignorance or accident. So far as the new puppy is concerned it is more important to avoid wrong associations than to attempt to create ones we want. Remember what I said about first associations and associations which are created when the animal's resilience is low. A young puppy is much more likely to forget an experience whether pleasant or unpleasant than an older one, but any animal is much more likely to get a bad fright in unfamiliar surroundings than in familiar ones.

Many dogs, I believe, have their temperaments completely ruined the first week they go to a new home as a result of the owner's misguided and often cruel attempts to house train them. A human baby is wrapped in nappies and even an older child is excused of wetting its bed if it is worried or upset, for example when he or she has to stay in a strange house. But a canine baby, which probably has never been in a house and which has been taken from its familiar environment by people it has never seen before, is expected to last all night without making a mistake. When it does it has its nose rubbed in it and probably smacked into the bargain. The owner then says 'I can't understand it. When I brought him home he was so friendly and rushed to greet me. Now he runs and hides every time he sees me'. What would you do if someone treated you like that?

Quite apart from the mental and physical suffering caused to the puppy this method has nothing to commend it. It is highly unlikely that the puppy will associate the punishment with the 'crime' which it could not avoid anyhow. There is, however, every likelihood that it will associate the punishment with the person who administers it and/or the place where it occurred. By persisting in this treatment it is possible to turn a normal bold puppy into a complete nervous wreck in less time than you could believe possible. I know dogs do survive this treatment with no apparent ill effects but they have exceptional temperaments in the first place.

The first object therefore should be to get the puppy to like you. And you can't make a dog like you any more than you can a person. All you can do is try to be a likeable person in the eyes of the dog by doing the things he likes. A young puppy likes being cuddled, fondled and petted, but not all the time. He wants to run about and play and chew things up. But you don't want him to chew the house to pieces so give him something to play with. Like all young animals he not only wants but needs to sleep. We all know how lack of sleep frays our nerves, making us irritable and bad tempered, but many puppies are kept continually awake because the owner wants to pet or play with them. Children are allowed, even encouraged to run around chasing a puppy often terrifying the life out of it. They give it no peace and one day they get bitten, which serves them right; but it is the puppy which is put down and the children are given another one to torment. If you can't train your children, it is unlikely you will train a dog. So, save it a lot of suffering by not having it at all.

These are only a few of the many examples of how unpleasant associations can be created by ignorance and lack of consideration. There can still be accidents. Small puppies, especially friendly ones, are adept at getting under one's feet and it is no good saying that it was his own fault that he got trodden on. A puppy does not reason like that and to him you are just an enormous animal towering above him with a huge foot which causes severe pain when plonked on top of him. There are lots of other things which can happen to puppies like doors being slammed on them and furniture falling on top of them, all of which can have a disastrous and sometimes lasting effect.

The best way to avoid unpleasant experiences to the puppy and at the same time save yourself some unpleasant experiences is to provide a play pen. This can be on the lines of a child's play pen and need not be elaborate or expensive. All that is necessary is an enclosure large enough to give a fair amount of freedom and strong enough to prevent the escape of the puppy in question. As there is so much variation in puppies and the conditions applying to different households I shall not attempt to describe the construction of a play pen. The puppy's bed should be placed in the pen. There is a wide variety of beds on the market, such as baskets, ideal for a puppy to chew to pieces. To the puppy an old tea chest or other box on its side is just as good if not better, as it is more enclosed. A board nailed across the front will stop any floor draught and help to keep in an old piece of blanket or other material for bedding. Some newspaper should be spread on the floor of the pen.

The advantage of a play pen should be obvious. While it not only prevents the creation of many undesirable associations of ideas, it also prevents the development of several bad habits. In very few households is there anyone with the time (even if they had the inclination) to keep a constant eye on a puppy. If he is in his pen he cannot mess on the best carpet, chew up the best slippers (they always choose the best ones), get trodden on or jammed in the door. Most important of all he won't get on your nerves or you on his.

If the puppy needs to relieve itself it will use the newspaper which can be picked up without any fuss and bother. Not that I advocate encouraging the puppy to use its play pen as a lavatory! The sooner a puppy is house trained the sooner it is likely to become a pleasant member of the household but there is rarely any need for drastic methods so often advocated. And no correction should be applied until the puppy is happy in its new surroundings and has complete confidence in its new owner. This may take an hour with an exceptionally bold puppy brought up in a house or perhaps two or three days with a less bold puppy reared in a kennel. An eight-week-old puppy should be completely confident in three days, if not there is something wrong either with the pup or the new home. Generally speaking the older a dog is the longer it will take to settle down and the more effect its previous upbringing will have. For instance, a pup reared from eight weeks in a home with children can at six months go to another home with children and settle down right away, but the same pup if reared in a home with a quiet elderly couple, or in kennels with a lot of other dogs, might never get over the shock of a house full of noisy children. We have found that one of the worst ages to change a puppy's environment is between four and five months old when it is teething.

To return to the question of house training few people realise that the average puppy wants to be clean in its own living quarters. All animals born in nests learn at quite an early age to go out of the nest to relieve themselves, thereby keeping their living quarters clean. The object should be to develop this instinct which can usually be done without any correction at all and certainly without the brutal treatment so often administered.

The first essential is an observant owner. Because of its instinct to be clean nearly every puppy will show symptoms of wanting to relieve itself. Unfortunately few owners recognise these symptoms and expect the puppy to ask to go out by whimpering or even barking. The most usual symptom is when the puppy simply starts looking around and probably sniffing the floor. When this happens take him out, wait until he has done what he has to do, praise him well and bring him back in. Don't just push him out and shut the door. He may well have decided that the door mat was the ideal place for his purpose and wait on the doorstep until the door opens, when he will come in and do what he intended doing exactly where he intended doing it. If you do catch a puppy actually in the act of squatting down pick him up firmly by the scruff say 'No' or 'Bad boy' in a corrective tone (the equivalent of his mother's growl) and take him out. To a young puppy this is *very* severe correction and should be done quietly without any shouting or flapping of folded newspapers so often recommended.

The important thing is to catch the puppy in the act and this rule applies to all training. Correction after the event (even seconds after) is unlikely to do any good and more than likely to do a great deal of harm. Remember that we are trying to work on the dog's mind and not his body and he will associate correction with what is on his mind at the time. For instance if a dog is corrected when he is looking at a cat with the obvious intention of chasing it that should be very effective. If he is corrected as he is chasing the cat that should be effective too. But if he chases a cat up a tree and you correct him when he returns to you, you will have corrected him for coming back, not for chasing cats. Thus many dogs are taught by their owners *not* to come back when called – and they still chase cats!

In the same way many puppies become afraid of owners who leave them alone for hours then return and punish them for wetting on the floor – which the poor little blighter could not avoid anyway. 'Of course he knows,' they say. 'Just see how guilty he looks.' But he does not look guilty at all, he simply looks afraid and with very good reason. You can prove this for yourself by scolding any reasonably sensitive dog when it has done nothing wrong and it will immediately look 'guilty' through fear or apprehension.

If one has to leave a puppy for a long period, put him in his play pen and of course he can sleep in it at night. All one has to do then is pick up the soiled newspaper. As he gets older he should learn to wait until he is let out and should be able to do so. A puppy accustomed to newspaper will sometimes prefer to use it in preference to going out. If you take it up and keep an eye on him you should notice when he goes looking for it and take that as a signal to let him out.

Our own dogs are never house trained in the generally accepted sense but simply encouraged to develop their instinct to be clean. Some live in the house and some in kennels and it is rare indeed for an adult to make a mistake

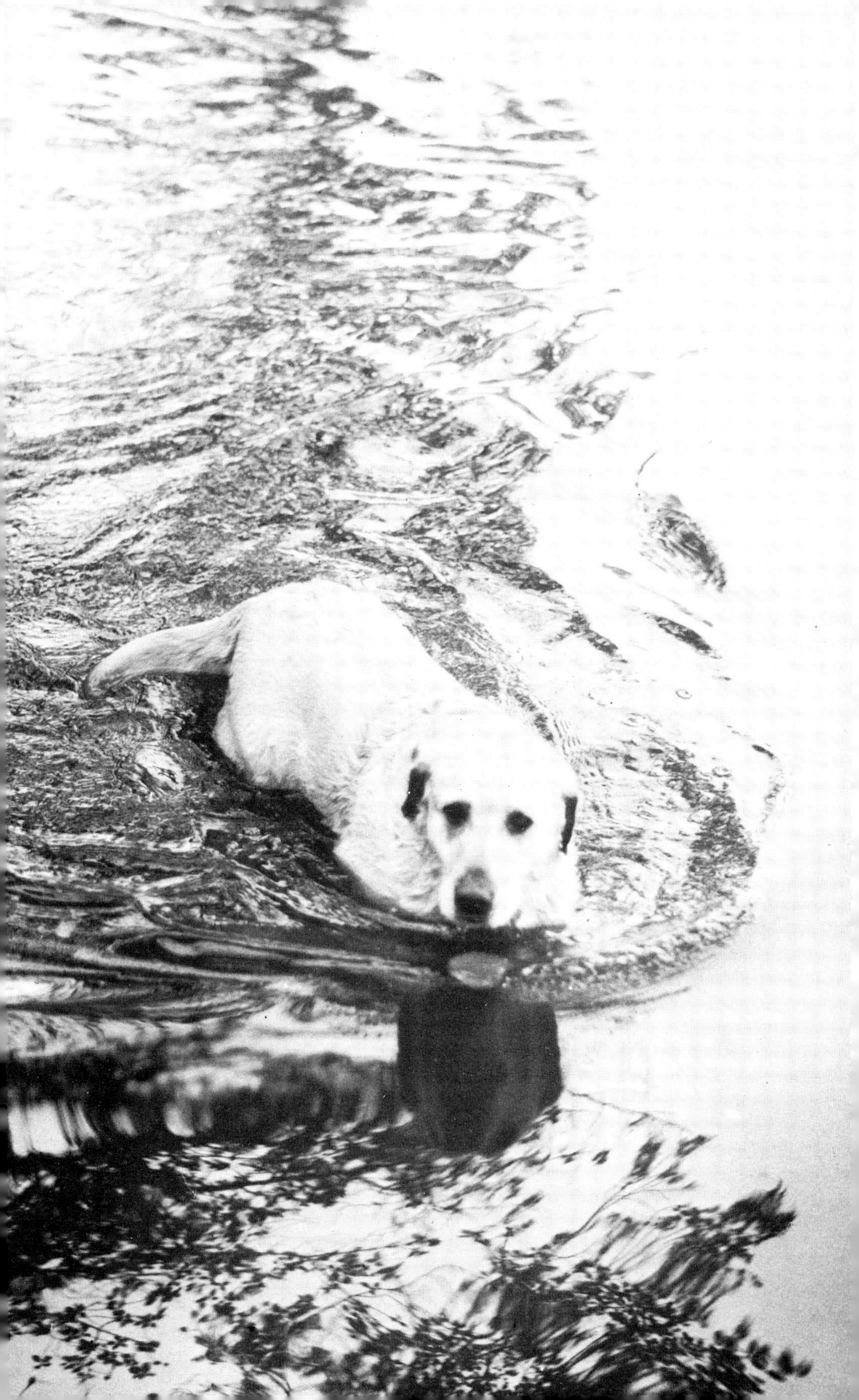

in either. They work in studios, live with us in a motor caravan and often stay in hotels and the only problem we ever have is when a director wants a dog to lift its leg in the studio! Having been encouraged to be clean very few of our dogs will do this indoors but will readily oblige outside on the studio lot.

Dog training cannot be divided into compartments and it is useless deciding to spend a fortnight on one exercise and then a fortnight on another. All training must synchronise and a lot of it has to take place simultaneously. There are however, certain 'exercises' which must be learnt before going on to other exercises. These are the basic exercises and the important point about them is that once the teacher and the pupil understand them thoroughly they can go on to more advanced exercises at any time – even after a lapse of several years. Space being limited I intend to deal only with the basic exercises. By the time you have mastered them I hope you will be keen enough on training to buy a book and proceed to more advanced training.

My reason for starting with house training is not because it is more important than other exercise or because it should be taught first. Indeed it is the only exercise which is of no benefit to anyone except the owner – or his friends who visit his house – which is probably why the average owner is so much keener on house training than on teaching the dog not to bite the postman! And that is why I started with it – because it is the first thing most people want to know about. There is actually another reason for starting house training soon after a puppy goes to a new home. A puppy with a strong instinct to be clean will soon choose a secluded spot as a 'loo' and will always go there. If that happens to be at the bottom of the garden it's fine. But if it happens to be behind the piano or the couch in the best room that's not so funny. And if an idea like that (based on an instinct) is allowed to develop it can be very difficult to change. All training must endeavour to create good habits and prevent bad ones.

One good habit which the puppy should learn right from the start is to come when called. In spite of everything you believe or have been told about dogs that 'understand every word said to him' dogs do not in fact, understand any words at all. They simply recognise sounds (far more accurately than we do) and they associate these sounds with certain actions. If your dog gets excited when you mention 'Walk' it is simply because he associates that sound (not a word to him) with going for a walk. Instead of recognising that simple fact dog owners resort to spelling the word. Very soon the dog associates the sounds W-A-L-K with going for a walk and his owners think he has learnt to spell!

At this stage we are mainly concerned with encouraging the puppy to come to us in response to a particular sound. The sound is usually the dog's name and where there are a lot of dogs, such as we keep, it is important that each and every one responds to its own name and to no other. But we do not go around repeating a dog's name over and over again for no reason at all. We use the dog's name when we want him to come to us – and if we don't want him we don't call him. The average owner, however, appears unable to desist from repeating the puppy's name every time he sees it. Not only that – the whole family, friends and neighbours will want to have cosy chats with any new puppy repeating its name over and over again in the process. Any new puppy we get will come to us in response to its name within a day or two but the average puppy hears its name so much that it completely ignores the sound just as it does the sound of the radio or television.

Constantly repeated sounds without association become ignored. For that reason it is often advisable to teach a dog to come to you in response to a different sound altogether like 'here' or 'come'. The word matters not and it is just as easy to teach a dog to come by saying 'go' as by saying 'come'. What does matter is that you always use the same command and use it in the right tone of voice. As I said earlier, a puppy instinctively cowers or even runs away at the sound of its mother's growl and will rush to greet her when she makes her soft welcoming noise, which is almost inaudible to human ears. The ability to change the tone of voice is vital in training and is one of the gifts which divides successful trainers into successful and unsuccessful. Don't confuse tone with volume. It is never necessary to shout at a puppy in the confines of its own house.

Now we come to the big question. How do you teach this charming puppy to rush to you in joyous bounds every time you call it? To start with you want to persuade rather than try to make it come. Later you may have to make him (he may have lost some of his charm by then!) but try persuasion first.

Obviously you should start by calling the puppy in a nice friendly persuasive tone of voice, never in a harsh correcting tone. If you stand straight up he is likely to stand back staring at the great thing towering above him but if you squat down he should come up to you even if you do not ask him.

A timid puppy will move away every time you move towards him but is almost certain to come nearer if you move away from him.

An outstretched hand with moving fingers will attract

nearly any puppy, and many adult dogs, while the same hand with fist clenched will be ignored. There is a general belief that one should always present the back of the hand to a strange dog. Working with dogs as I do in close contact with a great variety of self-styled dog lovers I find the efforts to carry out this exercise as amusing as it is unsuccessful.

Perhaps the commonest of all mistakes which people make in approaching a strange dog (and that includes a new puppy) is to stare at it. The only animal which likes its friends to look it 'straight in the eye' is the human being. Other animals do this only if they are afraid of each other or are about to attack. Watch two dogs meeting. If they look straight at each other you can expect a fight but if they approach shoulder to shoulder and walk stiffly round and round each other they will end up on friendly terms; so never stare at a new puppy when you are trying to get on friendly terms.

Now you are out in the garden with your pride and joy and you want him to come when called. He is probably sniffing around the gatepost or digging up the flower bed. Don't call him – for the simple and obvious reason that he won't come anyhow! An untrained puppy will do the thing which provides, or is likely to provide, the greatest pleasure at the time. Anyone who thinks that his voice is more attractive to a puppy than a hole in the ground or a smell on a gatepost has got the puppy's priorities wrong. Wait until the puppy appears to have nothing important to do and call it then. The best time is usually when he happens to be coming to you anyhow. Crouch down, hand extended, and call the puppy in a friendly persuasive tone. When he reaches you make a great fuss, fondle him and possibly offer a reward in the form of food. Do this several times when the puppy is sure to come and he will soon associate the sound of his name with the reward of food and/or petting. He will then have this association of ideas to strengthen the natural inclination to go to a friendly voice or hand. In most cases this combination will soon be strong enough to induce the puppy to leave the hole he is digging or the smell he is sniffing.

The mistakes most people make is in never calling the puppy unless he is doing something they don't want him to do – which is usually something he *does* want to do. Every time you call a puppy and he obeys you (even if he happened to be coming anyhow) you have gone a step forward. Every time you call him and he disobeys you you have gone a step back. And if you persist in calling him when he is certain to disobey you, you will actually teach him *not* to come when called. Whatever you do, never, under any circumstances, scold or correct a dog in any way when it comes to you – no matter how much you feel like murdering it!

Now we have a puppy which comes to you in response to reward alone. But he will only do so if the reward is better than the alternative – and dog's lives, like ours, are made up of alternatives. A puppy will probably find food and petting more rewarding than aimlessly digging a hole or sniffing round a gatepost. But if the hole leads to a stinking old bone previously buried there or, when the dog is a bit older, a bitch in season has been around the gatepost, cooing voice, outstretched hand and pocketfuls of titbits may prove to be a poor alternative. We must then resort to correction as well as reward to build up the association we want. It should be noted that correction is only resorted to when reward has failed.

Our puppy is back in the same hole and you call him as before. But this is a much more interesting hole and, if the puppy responds at all, it is merely to look up as if saying 'Hang on a minute, I'm busy'. Here we have a situation where it is very easy to correct the puppy as he is doing the wrong thing and you should always take advantage of such opportunities. You have *asked* the puppy to come by calling his name in a nice friendly tone and he has refused. Call his name again, this time *telling* him to come in a very firm tone. It is possible that the puppy may respond to this change of tone. If so, change your tone of voice and whole attitude completely, and reward him with enthusiasm. If he does not respond pick up a handful of earth or small gravel and call him again even more harshly. If he does not respond this time throw the earth or gravel at him. As this 'hail' descends on him from heaven he will almost certainly get a fright and look round for a protector – that's you! Call him to you, make a great fuss of him and do all you can to console him in his misfortune. The object is to get him to associate the harsh tone of voice with something nasty out of the blue. He must not know that you threw it and, if you do it properly, it is almost certain that next time he hears that harsh tone he will anticipate another 'hailstorm' and rush to you for protection – which you must always provide.

Never allow a puppy to run loose in a strange place until he will come to you every time you call him in the house or garden. Even then, you may find that when he sees another dog in the park he rushes off. I cannot over-emphasise the importance of nipping this habit in the bud and the best way for the novice is probably by using a check cord – about thirty feet of light cord attached to a dog's collar at one end with the other end in your hand. Let the puppy rush off and, as he nears the end of the cord call his name in a harsh tone. This time, instead of the handful of earth, the jerk on the check cord will provide the correction. He will probably do a somersault but don't worry. This method has been used by generations of gun dog trainers and I have never heard of a dog hurting himself. As he recovers from the jerk call him in a nice friendly tone and, when he reaches you, reward him lavishly. Never drag him to you. The line should be used as a means of correction when the dog tries to run away but you should encourage him to you by reward.

This method of training should naturally never be carried out until the dog is on a collar and lead and it is unlikely that a puppy will run after other dogs until he is about six months old. He will have to learn to go on a collar and lead before you take him out in public, and the place to teach him is not on the street or in the park but in his own garden or even indoors. Remember that a lead should never be regarded as a means of making a dog go with you but merely as a means of preventing him going too far away. Never put a collar and lead on a puppy until he will follow you without one.

There is a lot of argument about the best type of collar. Generally speaking, an ordinary buckled leather collar is as good as any for a puppy to start with. The puppy can be allowed to wear one and become quite familiar with it before the lead is put on. Start with a long lead and use it only to stop the puppy. Encourage him to come with you by rewarding him in the ways I have already described. Providing he will follow you without a lead (even if you do carry food in your pocket) he should soon follow you with one. It is more a question of familiarisation than actual training.

The usual problem is not how to get a puppy to go on a lead but how to stop him pulling once he has become familiar with it.

Here again this should be stopped before it becomes a habit, which is easier to prevent than to cure. It is important that when the puppy pulls you do not pull against him. Correct him for pulling with a sharp jerk on the lead and

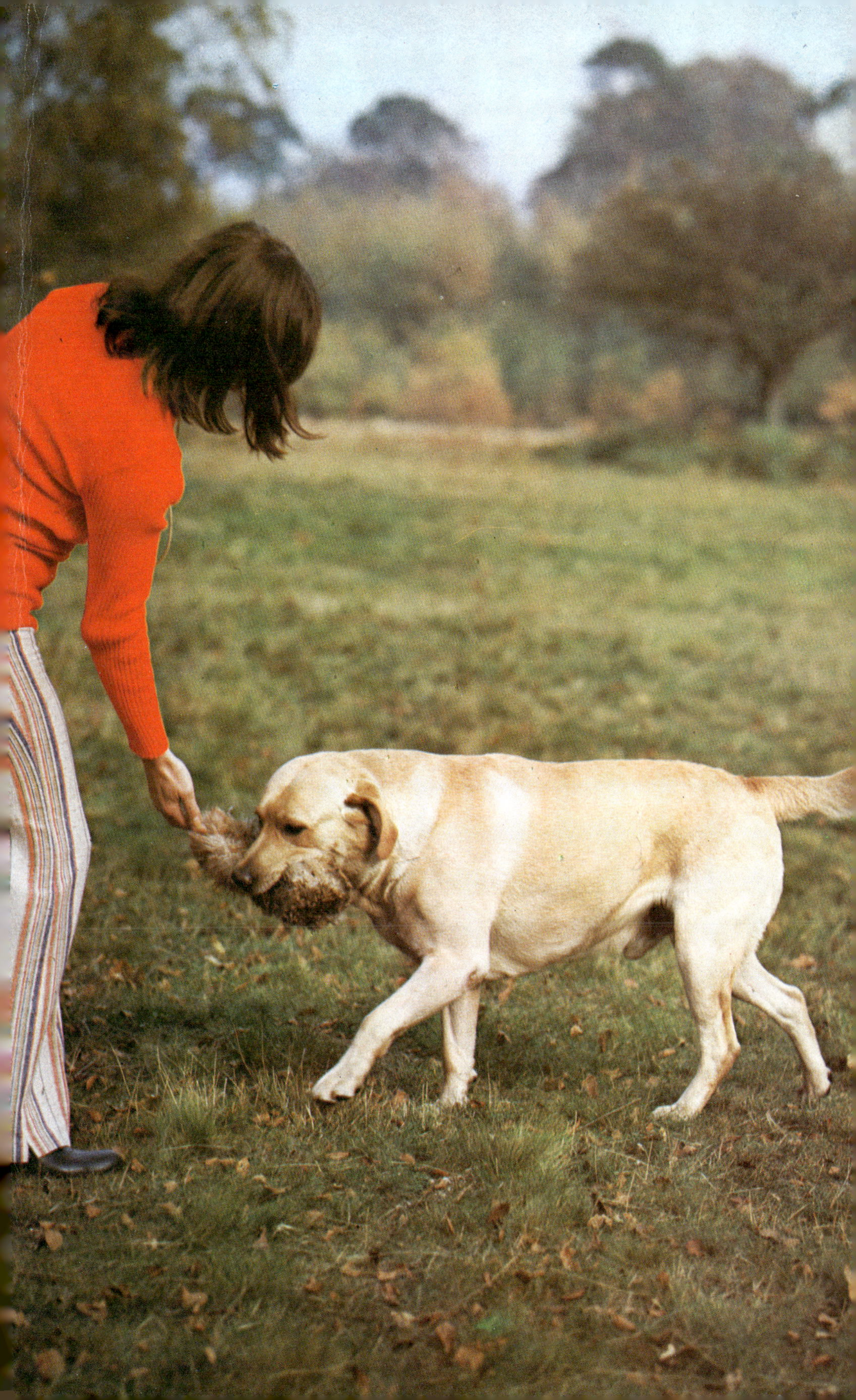

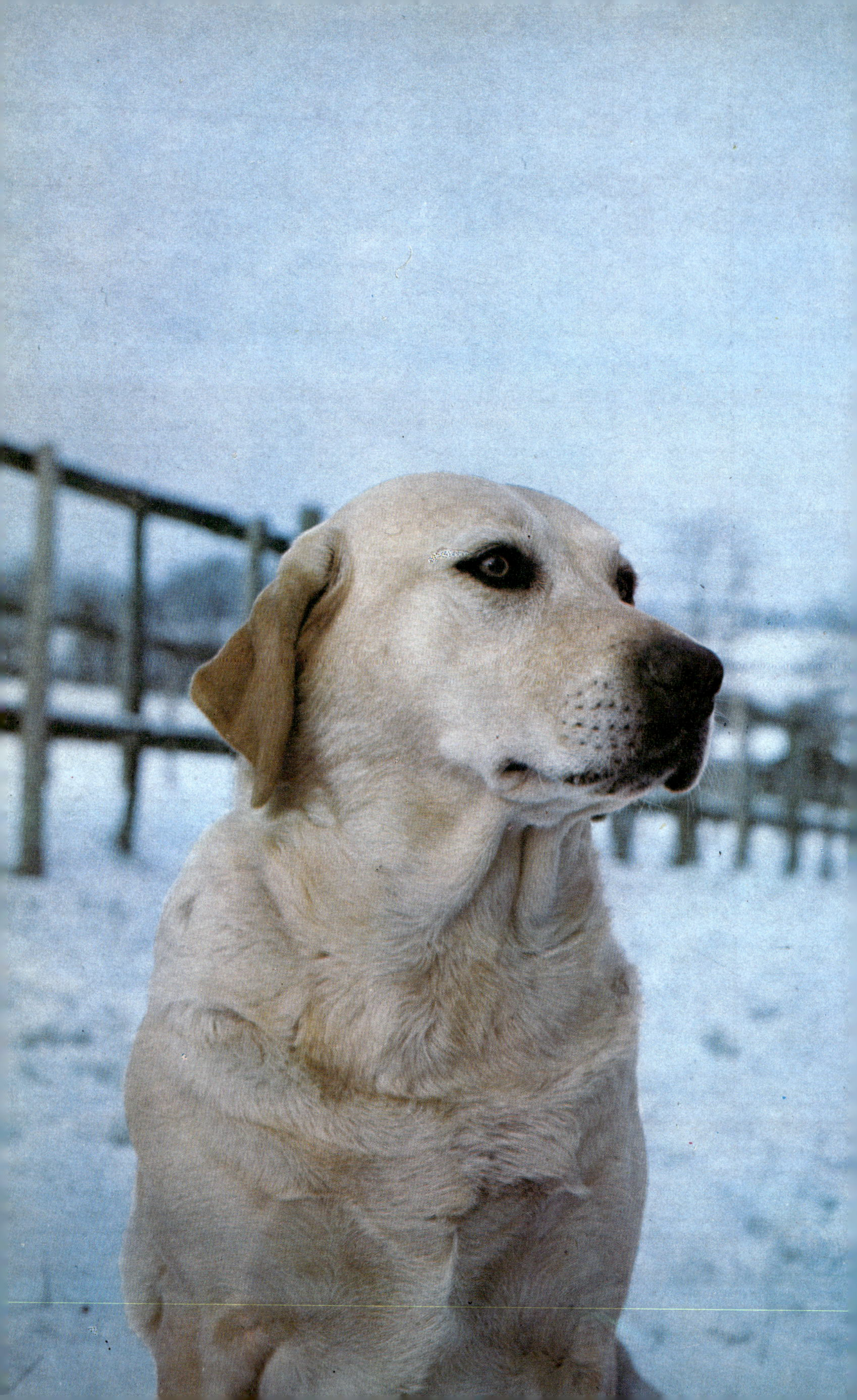

when he comes back to you in response, praise him well. Obviously you cannot jerk a dog on a short lead. For training a lead should be three or four feet long, pliable (we now use nylon web leads almost entirely), with a strong clip. If the puppy pulls, let the lead go suddenly and, before he has regained his balance, give him a sharp jerk. With a young puppy quite a small jerk will suffice, but it requires a considerable amount of skill and strength to cure an adult dog of pulling. There is little pleasure in taking out a dog which constantly pulls so, for your own sake as well as the dog's, don't let the habit develop.

If, in spite of your efforts, the puppy is pulling by the time he is six months old I would suggest taking him to a local training class. I have mixed feelings about training classes where one often finds the blind leading the blind – not very successfully either! I get a great many cries for help from dog owners and almost all of them have already attended training classes! Some of the advice given by self-styled experts is quite frightening. I have met many sensitive dogs with temperaments completely ruined by classes.

On the other hand I know many dogs and owners who have benefited beyond belief. Like many other successful trainers, I started by going to classes. It really all depends on the instructor who in this country (not in America) gives his services free. Unfortunately free advice is often worth just what it costs. My advice is to go along to a training class (the Kennel Club will give you a list of those in your area) without your dog and see whether dogs which have been attending for some time behave in the way you want your dog to behave.

You now have a puppy which is clean in the house, comes when you call it (and stays with you) and walks on a loose lead. The other important exercise to make him a pleasure rather than a nuisance is that he stays where he is told without bringing complaints from the neighbours. Here we must go right back to the beginning with the puppy in the play pen. If, when you leave him, he cries to get out and you take him out you will be rewarding him for crying. It is incredible how quickly a young puppy will learn that whenever it wants attention all it has to do is howl. The longer you stay with a puppy coddling and consoling him the longer he will whine or howl when you leave him. If you go away and leave him alone he will probably howl for a bit and then settle down and go to sleep. A puppy accustomed from the start to being left alone in his play pen is unlikely to create any problems when you come to leave him in the car or any other strange place.

If he does persist in howling or barking when left alone, put him in his pen or just shut him in a room and go away. Stop when you get out of sight and wait for the noise to start. When it does, go back quietly. The puppy won't hear you when he is making a noise but he will whenever he stops, so you must stop and wait until he starts again. The idea is to get right up to the door while he is actually making a noise, then open it suddenly (which will surprise him anyhow) grab hold of him and scold him severely. Now start all over again, and if he makes a noise repeat the whole process. It is unlikely that he will make a noise this time so wait a few moments (don't tempt Providence by waiting too long) and go back to him again. This time make a great fuss to reward him for being quiet.

The usual mistake people make is unintentionally rewarding the dog for making a noise. They say 'Now, now, be a good boy. Don't make a noise', or 'It's all right, Mummy's here. No need to cry about it', and they say it all in the most soothing and rewarding tone possible. Having been rewarded by tone of voice (probably by gentle stroking too) for barking or whining the dog naturally does it again, and again, and again for as long as he is rewarded. It is interesting to note that bad tempered owners never have problems of this sort. They don't wonder what to do or read books on the subject. The dog irritates them by making a noise and, as it is actually barking, is told in no uncertain terms to 'Shut up'. If it doesn't, it gets a hefty clout on the ear and next time it hears 'Shut up' it shuts up! That is not how I train dogs or believe that dogs should be trained but it is effective.

Your pup should now be clean in the house, come when

called (at any time and in any place) and be quiet when left on his own. And that is more than can be said for many of the dogs working in the Obedience Championships at Crufts! If you do aspire to more advanced training (and I hope some of my readers will) there are several books on the subject and plenty of people willing to offer advice.

JOHN HOLMES

An animal man if ever there was one, John Holmes was born and brought up on a farm in Scotland, and is the son of a famous breeder and exhibitor of Clydesdale horses and a judge of horses and cattle. As a boy he kept terriers who earned their keep by keeping the farm free of vermin. As an encore the terrier team entertained the farm workers and locals with a variety of party tricks. Later he graduated to training sheep- and cattle-dogs, using them for real work; he drove sheep ten miles to Perth market once a week, summer and winter, for a number of years.

He bought his first Corgi, Nippy of Drumharrow, in 1933 for two guineas, and later owned many famous Corgis. Mr Holmes took up obedience training after the war and in 1950 won the Junior Stakes at the ASPADS Trials; he then started training difficult and disobedient dogs for other people, and in no time at all became a prominent figure with a nationwide reputation.

In his own words, at this point he really began to learn about dogs and, more important, dog people. He ran dog training classes at Henley on Thames, and among other successes the instructor married his 'star pupil'. Together, Mr and Mrs Holmes built up a team of dogs who gave displays all over the British Isles – a mongrel from the team started his film career in 'Knave of Hearts'. This was quickly followed by a television series of dog programmes, 'Your Dog and Mine', for which John supplied the performers. Since then he has handled all sorts of other animals, including rats, on hundreds of films, television plays and commercials, and has appeared in numerous documentaries and discussion programmes on television. His film, 'A Tale of Two Puppies', was networked over all regions around Christmas 1970, and he has also made a seven-episode series for Southern Television called 'Training the Family Dog' based on his book *The Family Dog* (now in its fifth edition). Other books by John Holmes include *The Farmer's Dog* (about training sheep- and cattle-dogs) and *Obedience Training for Dogs*.

J.C.

5 Breeding
BY BETTY PENN-BULL

There is an old theory that every bitch should have a litter, but there seems to be no evidence to support this, so unless there is a definite desire to breed, the certainty of placing the resulting puppies satisfactorily, and the ability to provide the necessary care and attention, it is not advisable to embark on mating a bitch.

My opinion is that a bitch is best bred from either regularly or not at all, and that the single, so-called 'therapeutic' litter may well unsettle her, awakening the maternal and breeding instincts which are then subsequently thwarted if she is not allowed further puppies.

I have known many maiden bitches which have lived healthy lives into ripe old age, and I do not advise anyone to mate a bitch unless the puppies are really wanted. Never do so 'for her sake' and risk bringing puppies into the world for which it may be impossible to find good and suitable homes.

There are new opinions these days in regard to spaying bitches, and this now seems to be more acceptable than it used to be. But it is important that a bitch is fully developed before this is done, and she should have had at least one season in order to have reached complete maturity. Guide Dogs For The Blind use spayed bitches almost without exception, and this has not been found to affect their disposition, health, well-being or ability to work adversely.

Small breeds are usually easily controlled when in season, but with the larger ones, or where premises are not completely secure from invasion by trespassing dogs, spaying is certainly preferable to mis-mating and a subsequent unwanted litter.

Bitches used for breeding should conform to certain standards physically and mentally, and those falling short of these requirements should be discarded. They should be sound and healthy, of good type and conformation, and free from structural, organic or hereditary defects. In addition they should be of good temperament; nervous or bad-tempered stock should not be bred from. People sometimes appear to have the wrong ideas about breeding and I have heard remarks like, 'She is so nervous and excitable, I think a litter will steady her'; 'She keeps getting skin trouble, I hope having puppies will help to clear it up'. I feel this argument should be in reverse. Are these dogs suitable to be bred from? Do we want half a dozen more with poor temperaments or with some physical disability? If the answer is that we do not, then the simple solution is not to breed from such stock, and they should be excluded from one's breeding programme. The possibility of benefiting the parent at the expense of the unborn young is a wrong concept.

    Before being mated the bitch should be in top condition and perfect health. She should be well nourished on a properly balanced diet with ample protein, but it is preferable if she is a little on the lean side rather than slightly too fat.

Bitches normally come into season for the first time at about nine months of age, and thereafter at six monthly intervals. But there may be some variation in these times and this is not necessarily an indication of any abnormality. Small dogs in particular may have their first heat as young as seven or eight months of age, while larger ones may be a year old or even older. The cycle may vary too, and occasionally a bitch will go twelve months between seasons, while with some of the smaller breeds it may occur again after only four months' intervals. But if a bitch has three seasons in a year, one of these will not be fertile. Usually, after a litter the cycle adjusts and the times revert to the normal six months. When a bitch is due in season she should be tested each day with a swab of cotton wool pressed to the vulva to check for the first sign of colour. She can then be observed, and the pattern of her season noted.

As a rule, dogs tend to sniff around a bitch and show interest before the season actually starts, and this is often an indication that it is pending. But once the colour appears most dogs leave a bitch severely alone during the early period and I do not usually find it necessary to segregate her for at least six or seven days. After this time she must be carefully isolated.

Colour usually continues for about nine or ten days and then it gradually begins to fade, and by about twelve days, which is normally the height of the season, there is either just a pinkish tinge or it is practically colourless. As a rule the heat lasts for three weeks and the bitch must be kept isolated until the end of this period whether mated or not.

With some of the smaller breeds there is a more rapid cycle, the colour fades sooner and the bitch may be ready at eight or nine days, and the season completely over in fourteen or fifteen days. Some of the larger breeds may not be ready to mate until fourteen to sixteen days or even later, and their season may last twenty-four days, or occasionally even longer, so each bitch must be studied individually. It is important to note details of the first season as this can be helpful on subsequent occasions if a mating is intended.

With the smaller breeds the second season is a suitable time for mating, and this usually occurs at about fifteen months of age. But if a bitch is being shown, or it is not convenient, she can be left until later. It is advisable when possible to have her first litter by about three years of age while the frame is still elastic and has not hardened too much.

If a bitch is bred from regularly but has not been over-bred, I have known a number to continue having successful litters up to eight years of age. But it is important that she is maintained in good condition and receives the right care and attention.

It is not possible to generalise in regard to the frequency with which one can mate a bitch as each case must be assessed on its own merits.

As a rough guide the larger breeds which also tend to have larger litters may need a longer time between litters. With the smaller breeds one can often have two litters in succession and then miss a season without putting an undue strain on the bitch. But other factors come into account too, particularly the number of puppies produced and reared. If a bitch had seven or eight and reared all I would rest her a year before the next litter. But if she had only three or four I would consider mating her at her next heat. This would apply during the prime of her life, between two and six years old, but after six years of age I would not breed from her more than once a year.

Other factors must be considered too, such as her general health, condition and activity and whether she is an easy whelper. Some dogs of seven are like four-year-olds, and others are like ten-year-olds, so all these matters must be taken into account.

Arrangements should be made well in advance with the owner of the selected stud dog, and it is customary for her to visit him. A provisional date should be fixed as soon as she starts in season which can be varied later if necessary.

If the bitch is sent by rail she should be despatched two or three days before the height of her season and in consultation with the owner of the dog. She should be sent in a secure and comfortable box, properly labelled and with careful arrangements for her collection.

If she is taken personally which is preferable whenever possible, it is important the timing is correct to ensure maximum prospects of a successful outcome, and this entails the careful assessment of the vital factors of the timing, colour and her reactions. On arrival the bitch should be allowed a free run to relieve herself, to stretch her legs and to settle down a little after her journey, before being introduced to the dog. The actual mating procedure is dealt with under the section concerned with the stud dog.

After mating, the bitch must be kept segregated until the completion of her season, and she can then resume her normal life.

Care of the Bitch In Whelp

The bitch in whelp should be well cared for, but not coddled. For the first few weeks she may carry on with her ordinary routine providing this does not entail any excessive exertion. But she will be all the better for plenty of freedom and exercise, interspersed with adequate rest periods. She should not be allowed to get cold or wet, and should also be protected from excessive heat.

During the last few weeks several short walks are preferable to one long one, but she should be encouraged to keep active with gentle exercise until the end, although avoiding anything unduly strenuous. She should have as much liberty as possible and should not be closely confined except for minimal periods.

Feeding the in-whelp bitch may vary to some degree. With the small breeds, and with some which are not always easy whelpers, great care must be taken not to over-feed, and the aim is to produce small, strong puppies at birth, as larger ones may well be the cause of trouble at whelping time.

I feed as usual for the first six weeks, but I do ensure there is an ample meat ration, plus a limited amount of biscuit and raw or cooked vegetables. I give two equal meals for the last three weeks, increasing the meat allowance but decreasing the starch to a minimum. I give cod liver oil daily, but this is the only additive my bitches in whelp receive as they are a breed which are not always easy whelpers, so I ration them carefully. I do not add calcium or bone meal, or give milk or eggs or other extras.

But with many other breeds, and particularly the larger ones, it will be advisable to step up the rations after mating, and probably to provide various additives too, as this particular problem of whelping does not apply in all cases.

The big breeds usually have larger litters and the puppies are proportionately smaller at birth in relation to the size of the dam. So within certain limits the breeder must be guided by the needs of the individual bitch in deciding on the correct policy.

I give a small teaspoonful of liquid paraffin daily during the last week. I also give the bitch a thorough grooming and overhaul several days before the litter is due. This consists of a good brushing and combing into every corner. She is then sponged over with a cloth wrung out in weak Dettol and warm water, paying particular attention to the feet, under the body, the head, between the legs and under the tail. The anal gland is checked and cleared if necessary. The eyes and ears are examined and treated if required, and the mouth and teeth are inspected and cleaned if necessary.

Any excessive hair round feet, tummy and other parts may be tidied up if desired, but although I have a breed with furnishings I do not remove them from my bitches. Some breeders do, and this is a matter for the individual to decide.

The Whelping Quarters

The bitch should be introduced to the place where she is to whelp some days before the event, so she feels settled and relaxed there. This should be a quiet room or building, or an enclosed pen where she has privacy and is not worried by other dogs or by children or strangers.

The whelping box should be placed here, and it should be roomy enough for her to lie full length and still allow a margin of space beyond this. It should be raised on low slats to allow air to circulate beneath the base. There should be a removable board to slot into the front, but this should be taken out before whelping to avoid any risk of injury when the bitch goes in and out of the box. The sides of the box should be high enough to protect the bitch and puppies from draughts and a removable lid is an advantage.

A crush barrier should be provided which can be inserted into the box, with a clearance of two or more inches from the ground, and two or more inches from the sides of the box, according to the size of the dog, to avoid the possibility of the puppies being pressed behind the dam, and perhaps suffocated. This is similar to the pig-rail used for farrowing sows and provides a safe alley-way while the puppies are small. This barrier should not be put into position until after the bitch has finished whelping and it can be removed when the puppies are two or three weeks old, when they require more room and will be stronger.

I use an infra-red lamp for my litters and this is positioned across one corner of the box, so there is a warm spot for the puppies, but the opposite corner is cool if the dam prefers to lie there.

My whelping box has vinyl on the floor and this is then covered with several layers of newspaper and finally a thick blanket for the bitch and litter.

The Whelping

Bitches carry their young for sixty-three days, but this is subject to some variation. It is quite usual for a bitch to whelp three days early, while some of the smaller breeds may have their puppies five days before time. Puppies born more than five days early have a limited chance of survival. Some bitches may go overtime, but if this extends more than two or three days there is some cause for concern and there may be trouble ahead.

The first indication that whelping may be imminent is a drop in temperature which will fall below 100° (normal temperature in the dog is 101·4°). This may occur two or three days before the actual whelping, but when the temperature drops to 98° or 97° the whelping will generally occur within twenty-four hours.

The preliminary signs are restlessness, trembling, yawning, panting, bed-making, and possibly vomiting. Food is usually refused, and there is often a desire to pass water frequently.

All these symptoms may be present, or only some, and they may last for some hours, or even intermittently for a full day or more. But the whelping as such does not really commence until the contractions begin, so until that time it is a matter of waiting for further developments.

If there is a rise in temperature or a black or green discharge, trouble is indicated and veterinary advice must be sought without delay.

But if all appears normal do not interfere unnecessarily, but allow the bitch the opportunity to whelp. Some are slower than others, and it sometimes pays to be patient providing there are no abnormal symptoms.

Many bitches like the comfort of their owner's presence at this time, and a reassuring word and a little fondling will encourage them. Firm, but gentle stroking down the back is sometimes helpful in stimulating the contractions.

The bitch should not be fussed or agitated and the owner should remain calm and cheerful. The bitch can be offered glucose and milk or glucose and water from time to time, or she may be given a little brandy or whisky, but she should not have any solid food during whelping as this may cause vomiting.

The first puppy may appear quite quickly once the contractions start, or it may not come for two or three hours, or even more in some cases, as some bitches are much slower than others.

It is sometimes difficult to decide at what stage assistance should be given, and if an owner is a complete novice it is helpful to have an experienced breeder available who can advise in the event of any queries or difficulties or suggest when professional help is necessary.

The puppy should arrive head first, contained in its sac and with the afterbirth attached, and the dam should quickly release the puppy, cleaning it thoroughly and eating the afterbirth. But some bitches, particularly maidens, are slow at freeing the puppy's head, and in this case the breeder must do so without delay or fluid will get into the puppy's lungs and this may be fatal. The bitch should then be encouraged to lick and massage the puppy. If it is slow in breathing it should be rubbed and shaken and any fluid drawn from the nose and mouth; warmth is very important in helping to revive it.

The flat-nosed breeds are not usually able to attend to their newly-born whelps, and the attendant must be prepared to assist them by removing the puppy from the bag and severing the cord. The puppy should then be offered to the dam for her to clean and lick. If several puppies are born in rapid succession it may be advisable to remove some of the earlier ones temporarily and place them in a warm box away from the dam until the whelping is completed so that the newer arrivals can receive more attention, and the earlier ones do not get cold and neglected. But if this upsets the dam they must be left with her and endeavours made to keep them warm and dry. I use thick newspapers for the whelping and old sacks or blankets, and I put in more paper or old towels as we go along, to try and keep the bed as clean and dry as possible.

When the whelping is finished one person should take the bitch out to make herself comfortable. Meanwhile, a second person should gently lift out the puppies, then remove the soiled bedding, wipe round the box and put in fresh paper and a clean blanket. The anti-crush frame should then be inserted, the front board slotted in and the puppies replaced. The dam should then be allowed back, to find everything ship-shape, thus avoiding her being agitated by a lot of commotion going on around her.

She should be offered a warm drink and then left quietly to rest for a few hours, although it is generally wise to keep an unobtrusive eye on her to make sure all is well. I leave a small light for the first few days as I prefer a dull emitter lamp over the bed.

Post-Natal Care and Feeding

For the first few days after whelping it is important to check the bitch's mammary glands regularly. Run the hands lightly over all her teats and these should be soft and yielding. If one or more are hard and congested this indicates the puppies are not suckling from these, and this may result in milk fever or an abcess, so steps must be taken immediately to alleviate the condition.

The trouble is more likely to occur with small litters when the puppies are obtaining adequate milk supplies without drawing on all the teats. Those most likely to be affected are the back ones which often carry heavy milk yields, and to a lesser extent the front ones may also be affected. The middle breasts do not seem as likely to be involved and are usually those most readily drawn on by the puppies.

As soon as the condition is diagnosed the affected breast should be gently massaged and softened with warm poultices to ease the pressure. Then some of the milk should be drawn off, and when it is flowing freely one of the strongest puppies should be placed on the teat and encouraged to suck. When he has had his fill he should be replaced by another until the breast is clear.

There may be no further trouble once it is soft and pliable, and the puppies may now use it normally. But it must be watched and the treatment repeated if necessary. Once a gland becomes really congested and hard the puppies will avoid it as they are unable to draw the milk from it in this condition, so it is essential to get the milk flowing to avert any possible complications. The dam must also be kept under careful observation to ensure there are no complications as an aftermath of the whelping. Any rise in temperature, refusal of food, vomiting, unhealthy discharge, or diarrhoea should alert the breeder.

There may be retention of a puppy and if this is dead professional help must be summoned without delay; or perhaps the bitch has failed to pass one or more of the afterbirths, in which case an injection to encourage this may be called for, or antibiotics may be necessary. So it is essential to seek advice immediately if any abnormal symptoms such as these should occur.

If there is no infection and no complications, the bitch will usually be happy and relaxed after the birth, and ready to take nourishment, so any signs of discomfort or distress should cause the breeder to suspect something to be wrong, and he should therefore take the necessary steps to obtain advice or help should any untoward symptoms manifest themselves.

Once the puppies are safely born the bitch should be fed generously and this applies to nursing mothers of all breeds as suckling puppies imposes a great strain on the dam.

I give fluid feeds only for the first twenty-four hours. Then for the next twenty-four hours I add semi-solids such as fish, minced meat and eggs. If all is going normally I then gradually revert to ordinary food, simultaneously increasing the quantity given. From about a week after whelping until the puppies are weaned the dam will be fed lavishly with plenty of flesh (raw meat, stewed beef, ox-cheek, offal, sheep's head, paunch, fish, etc.), milk feeds of various kinds, eggs, broth, wholemeal food and vegetables. She also has calcium and cod liver oil, or similar additives.

If the litter is a large one I give three meat feeds and two milk meals during this period. If there are only a few puppies less food will be required, but this must be judged by the bitch's and the puppies' condition and her milk supply. Leave fresh water always available as nursing mothers require ample liquids.

Weaning the Litter
I like to start weaning puppies early to lessen the strain on the dam, and also to make this as gradual a process as possible. Scraped raw beef and enriched milk can be offered at the third week, and at four weeks puppies can be having two small feeds of each of these each day. Other items are then introduced gradually: cooked meat of various kinds, fish, and a variety of milk feeds, plus fine puppy meal or crumbled wholemeal bread. I also add cod-liver oil and calcium or their equivalents daily.

At five weeks mine have five meals a day, three of meat and two milk meals and I continue this until they are eight or ten weeks old. At five weeks I consider puppies to be fully weaned, but the dam is still allowed to visit them if she wishes to, but is never compelled to be with them. In fact from the time of the birth the dam is always free to get out of the box and away from the puppies if she wishes to do so.

Worming and Other Matters
Puppies should be wormed at least twice before sale, and they should not go to their new homes younger than eight weeks old. They should always be accompanied by a diet chart and instructions as to correct care and routine should also be given to the new owner.

Some breeds seem especially subject to worms despite every possible precaution. With my breed I find it necessary to dose at about three weeks old and again ten days later, with perhaps a third worming at about eight weeks old. But other breeds appear to be less susceptible, and it may be possible to defer the first worming until five or six weeks old, followed by a second dose a week or so later. One point I have observed is that puppies from maiden or young bitches seem to be much more liable to heavy worm infestation, and that as the dams grow older their progeny do not seem to be affected to the same degree.

Indications of worm infestation in young puppies are coat standing on end, hard and distended stomach, unhealthy motions, passing jelly or mucus, and a lack of weight gain. These symptoms may develop at a very early age and it is then advisable to dose without delay. The modern preparations are safe and effective and no fasting is required, and I have found no risk or danger involved in the treatment. Worming does not give puppies permanent immunity but they should remain clear for some weeks, although it may be advisable to repeat the treatment when they are about four months old, and subsequently as and when it appears necessary.

A further point is to keep puppies' nails short and they should be clipped each week to prevent them scratching the dam or catching in the bedding.

If tails must be docked and dew-claws cut these should be done a few days after birth. It is not a difficult job, but it is advisable for the novice to obtain the help of an experienced person to undertake this task. Care should be taken that tails are docked to the correct length as this varies for different breeds.

Some Aspects Concerning Dogs

Only suitable males should be used for breeding, and in addition to the same general requirements of good health and temperament which apply to bitches, the standards required regarding type and quality should, if possible, be even higher. Fewer males are required in a breeding programme, so the elimination process must be even more stringent. With working dogs the same rules of strict selection should also apply.

Those dogs which do not measure up to the desired standard should not be used at stud, and it is a mistaken conviction to assume that every dog should be mated.

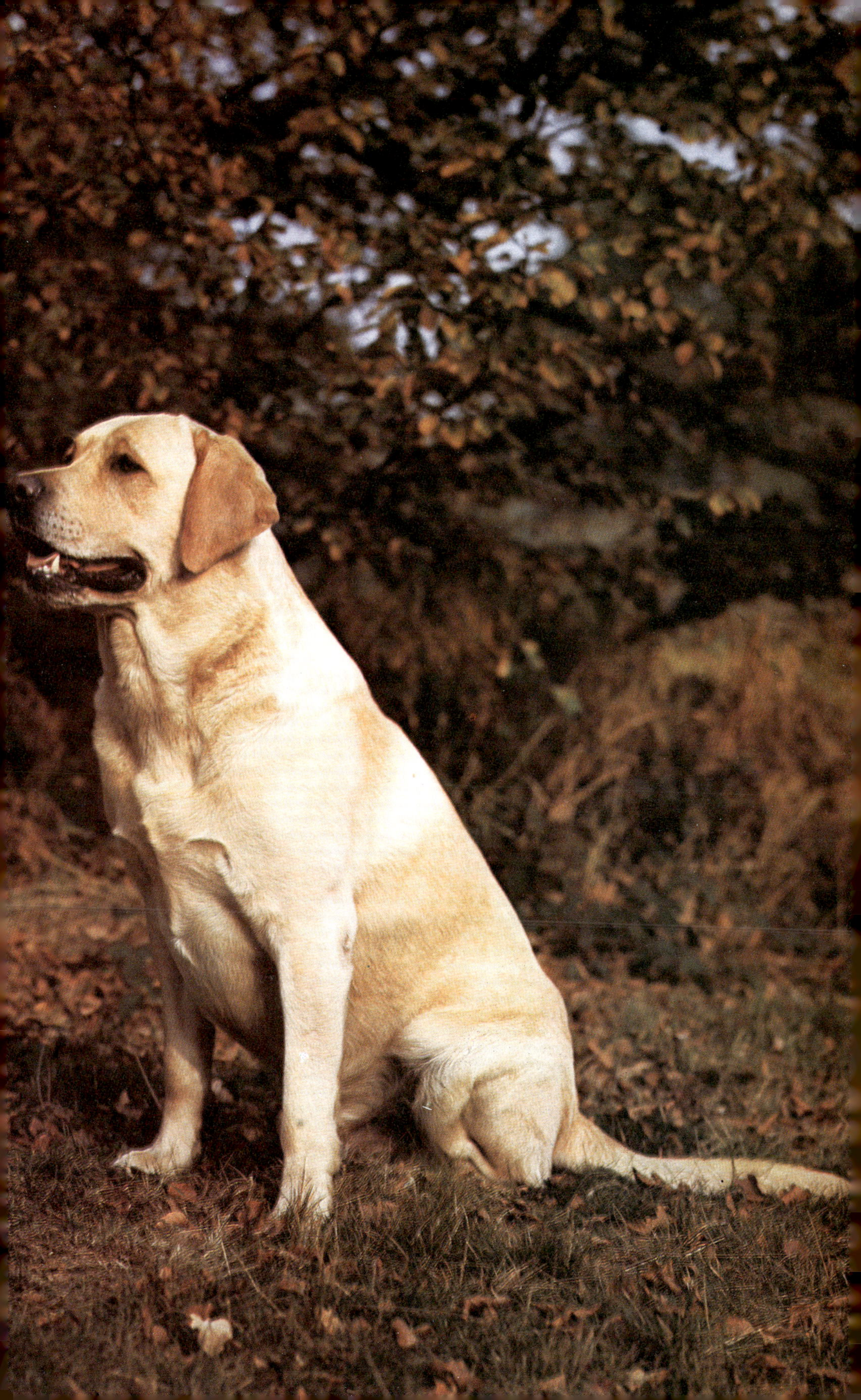

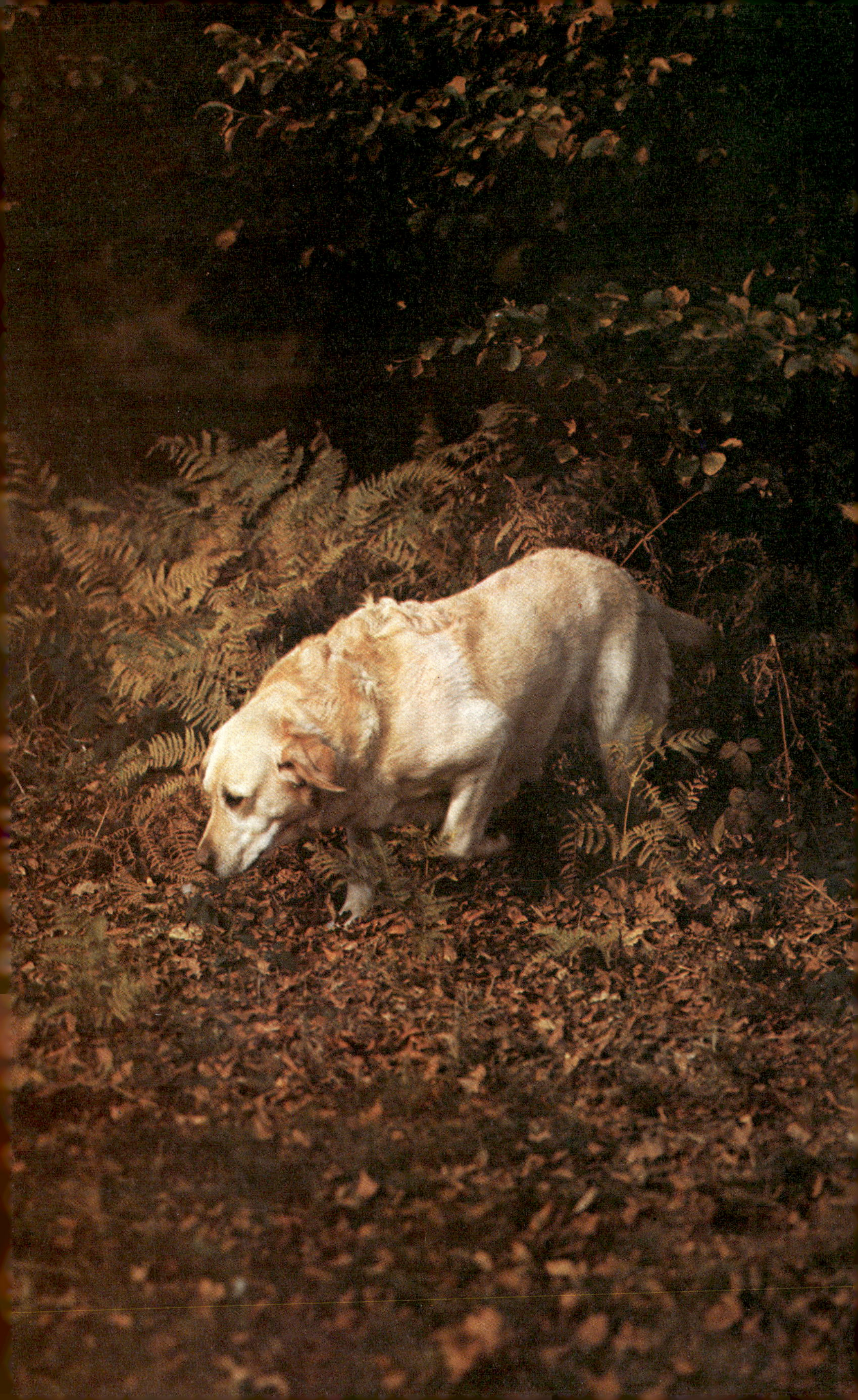

Apart from other considerations this would not be practical, for numbers would get completely out of control in the dog population, with a rapid increase in 'also-rans' and unwanted puppies.

If a dog is used regularly at stud he generally falls into a pattern of life and does not worry unless a bitch is ready for mating. But a dog which is used only once or twice during his life tends to become awakened but not satisfied, and may well be more frustrated than if not used at all.

Most males settle down after puberty and do not worry unduly, but some breeds or individuals tend to be more highly sexed than others, and if a dog becomes an embarrassment the question of castration should be considered. This course is not generally necessary but in extreme cases it may be the best solution. The worried owner of an oversexed dog may feel that if only he were mated it would calm him, but it will not generally solve any problems and as already suggested the condition will probably be aggravated.

So my advice is that you should accept that your dog will fall into one of three categories: firstly, top dogs to be used for breeding, secondly, other dogs which are kept for various purposes – as companions, as guards or for work. These dogs to remain entire, but not used at stud, and thirdly, dogs which are not suitable for breeding, but which are difficult and where castration may be advisable.

Care of the Stud Dog
A dog used regularly at stud must be kept in good condition, fit, hard and active. He should not be over-weight, but must be generously fed with a good proportion of protein in his diet. The frequency with which a dog may be used will vary according to a number of factors. Perhaps as a rough guide, the smaller and medium breeds might average two matings a week during the dog's prime when between two and six years old, and this should not tax him unduly. With younger dogs, under two years old, perhaps once a week would be wiser, and the same would apply to those over six years of age. But such suggestions are subject to variation and must be elastic. I have known of dogs used

much more frequently without apparent ill effects. With the bigger breeds it would not generally be advisable to use them as frequently as the smaller ones, but the question does not generally arise since they are not usually bred on a large scale in any case.

External considerations of management, handling, condition and the individual dog's potency, etc., must all play their part. If a dog is well cared for and is healthy and virile he may retain his fertility until he is in his 'teens; but this is unusual and not many dogs are still useful at stud after nine or ten years of age.

If a dog mates quickly and easily he can be used much more frequently than another, which requires several attempts to achieve a mating. The latter can lose more energy over one unsuccessful effort than the former would do in mating two or three bitches.

If a dog mates without trouble he will not be exhausted and will be as fit as before; after a little rest he will be ready to enjoy his food and be back to normal. If well managed a dog can be in regular use at stud and still keep in top condition for the show ring.

But conversely, the dog which steams about for prolonged periods, trying ineffectively until he is exhausted, panting and wild-eyed, and with his heart racing, will be far more spent. He is frustrated and upset and probably will not eat or rest, and these sessions if embarked on frequently will soon take their toll of a dog's condition.

The Mating

It is best to start a dog at stud when young as this is more likely to ensure an easy mating, and this could be at about ten months to a year old for a small dog and perhaps eighteen months or so for a large one.

It is preferable to commence a maiden dog with a steady and experienced brood bitch, as a nervy or snappy one can upset a youngster. A small, empty, enclosed area is usually best for the mating, where the dogs are not distracted, and where there are no obstructions to impede matters or to make the dogs inaccessible if help is necessary.

Usually two people should be present, one to concentrate

on the dog and the other on the bitch. But sometimes with big powerful dogs or those which are obstreperous, extra help may be required to steady the animals.

The bitch should be on the lead so she is under control, but she should be allowed free play to encourage the dog, and meanwhile the dog should be allowed to make advances and to gain confidence. The bitch must be the focal point and the handlers should remain background figures. Encouragement and praise may be offered, but these should be given quietly so as not to divert the dog's main interest from the bitch.

On no account should the dog be scolded or curbed, and no anger or irritation should ever be apparent during a mating or potential mating. If the bitch is aggressive she must be controlled, but this must be done by calming and soothing her, and by firm handling, or if necessary by muzzling her, and on no account by roughness or violent actions.

It is most important that matings are carried out in a tranquil atmosphere so a dog retains his confidence. If he is subjected to harshness or to inconsistent treatment, or is frightened or upset in any way, he may become an unreliable stud dog, easily discouraged, and reluctant to co-operate with his handler.

It is my considered opinion that many potentially valuable stud dogs are lost to their breeds, or have restricted opportunities because of mishandling, so it is very important to approach the situation sympathetically.

Sometimes a bitch may suffer from a stricture which makes the mating difficult, or even impossible, so if the dog appears to be striking correctly but does not achieve a 'tie', the bitch should be examined to test if the passage is clear. The small finger, first sterilised and then covered with a little petroleum jelly as a lubricant, should be gently inserted into the passage.

If the way is clear the finger will slip in easily, but if an obstruction is felt it will be necessary to stretch this, or break it down, to enable the dog to penetrate. This can generally be done by easing the finger in with a screwing action, gently pressing and twisting and working it to and fro. The stricture may consist of a strip of skin across the passage which will require stretching or breaking down, or it may be a thickened band ringing the passage which will need enlarging to allow a way through. If this treatment is carried out slowly and carefully it does not upset the bitch, but on no account must it be done roughly.

When the bitch shows signs of being prepared to accept the dog, by turning her tail, and if the dog tries to mount her, the handlers should be ready to assist if required. The one assigned to the bitch should steady her and should be prepared to hold her firmly with both hands should she jerk as the dog is mating her. Meanwhile, the other handler should be watching the dog, ready if necessary to give him some support if he shows signs of slipping away from the bitch before he has effected the mating. Once he is mated he should be kept on the bitch's back for a minute or two before being allowed to turn, as if not fully 'locked' he may come away if he turns too quickly.

With some of the smaller dogs it is customary not to turn them, but they are held on the bitch's back until the completion of the tie. With some of the larger ones it is usual to lower the dog beside the bitch as this seems more comfortable for many big dogs. But most make a complete turn and remain back to back during the mating, and this is the normal position. The length of the tie may vary from five or ten minutes to half an hour or more, but its duration has no relation to the results.

As they separate after mating I usually raise the bitch's hindquarters and gently tap the vulva which stimulates the contraction of the vaginal muscles. As the dogs part there is sometimes quite a back flow of fluid from the bitch, and I try and avert this as far as possible. Only a small amount of semen is required to fertilise the bitch but there is nothing to lose by taking what precautions one can!

If everything is normal with a satisfactory tie, one mating should be sufficient. But if there are any unsatisfactory aspects, such as the bitch coming into colour again, causing doubts as to the correct timing, if the tie was not a good one, or if perhaps she has a history as an unreliable breeder, then it may be wise to have a second mating.

If a bitch is difficult to get into whelp it is worth trying several spaced matings at three or four day intervals. Try the first one as early as possible, perhaps at seven or eight days; a second one at the normal time of perhaps eleven or twelve days, and another as late as possible, perhaps at fifteen or sixteen days. I have known bitches which do not follow the regular pattern, and which may require mating very early or very late to ensure conception, and this condition may be difficult to recognise and is only discovered and corrected by trial and error. But if a bitch is difficult to get into whelp it is worth trying varying the timing to endeavour to catch her at her most fertile period.

Sometimes there is a difference in height between the animals and it may be necessary to adjust this with a low platform. Usually it is the dog who requires raising, and a board (if necessary on blocks) may be used, preferably covered with a sack or a piece of carpet to give purchase.

Some breeders prefer to mate the smaller dogs on a bench or table and the dog soon becomes accustomed to this. Personally I prefer to mate them on the floor as I find it a natural sequence from the preliminary flirting, but this is an optional decision.

The bitch should be brought to the stud dog when she is ready for mating, and every effort should then be made to effect this. This is particularly necessary if a dog is young and valuable and likely to be in much demand at stud, for it is important to ensure he does not waste his energy and that he is not disappointed, which may undermine his confidence and determination. If a dog is brought in and out to a bitch which may or may not be ready, and if he is tried repeatedly and unsuccessfully, these abortive attempts can be most damaging to his future career at stud. Whereas if he is only introduced to bitches ready for mating and is given correct assistance, culminating in a successful outcome, he is likely to be fully co-operative and ready to tackle even the most difficult bitch, and he should become virtually one hundred per cent reliable.

It is most important that the bitch is never allowed to bite the dog, and this is even more vital with a youngster. If a dog is roughly treated by a bitch in his early days, this may affect him to the extent that he refuses to go near any other bitch which even growls, so the handler of the bitch must keep her under control and be sure that this does not happen.

If a young dog mounts the bitch incorrectly he must not be checked or restrained in any way but the bitch should be manoeuvred around towards him, and he should still be praised and encouraged. To check him would not imply 'Don't do it at that end – do it at this end' – it would simply mean 'Don't do that'.

I once had the greatest difficulty in handling a young dog whose owner had been 'training' him by giving him a slap every time he tried to mount the bitch at the wrong angle, at the same time scolding him and telling him what a silly dog he was, and that was not the right way to do it. Eventually I had to send her right away, out of his sight and sound as he was thoroughly bewildered by her apparently wanting him to mate the bitch and then giving him a smack when he tried to do so.

Sometimes a dog is shy and very reluctant to try to mate a bitch if people are near, but he does eventually succeed when running with her and while both are free. In this event it is wise to go quietly towards them once they are mated and to hold the dog gently, stroking and praising him quietly, and making relaxed contact, so he becomes accustomed to human proximity in these circumstances, and he may thus be willing to accept help on a subsequent occasion if the necessity arises.

Dogs running together may mate naturally sometimes, but sooner or later there will be problems and it may not be possible for the dog to effect the mating without some assistance. Either there may be a big difference in size between the animals which will require adjustment, or the bitch may jerk away at the crucial moment and require steadying. So unless the dog will accept human help, there will come a time when he may fail, so it is important for the breeder to accustom him to being handled.

After the mating the bitch should be shut away quietly for a rest before she is exercised or travels, and I try to avoid her passing water too soon. The dog too, should be put in his bed to relax and unwind for a period, and he should not be returned among other dogs for some time until he has completely settled down, when he can resume his normal life. If he is returned too quickly among other males this may create tension and such mishandling may well precipitate friction.

Final Hints on Management
I have kept stud dogs for many years, and I do not consider that they should be treated any differently from other dogs in their ordinary life, and my experience is that if they are treated normally they will respond normally.

But there are certain aspects which require careful management, and it is important not to inflame possible latent jealousy by allowing situations involving tension to occur.

Well before a bitch reaches the height of her season she

must be removed and kept completely away from all stud dogs. If several dogs are running together and are able to see, or sniff, a bitch in season this will understandably cause friction, and possibly aggression and trouble.

I always run my dogs together, and have had as many as six or seven or more mature males mixing freely with each other and an equal number of bitches, all happy and friendly together, and I think when this can be managed dogs are much more contented and well adjusted.

It is sometimes considered that a stud dog must not mix with bitches or he will not mate them, but this has not been my experience, and I have had many very successful stud dogs who have lived as family pack dogs.

But although stud dogs may run together under supervision and in open areas, they should never be confined in small enclosures without somebody in attendance.

Young males of the same age which grow up together may not agree well when mature, as neither may be willing to accept the dominance of the other. But I have found if I grow on one new youngster at a time there is not this problem, as he automatically falls into his position as the junior member of the pack, and is thus integrated into the group. The next new addition to follow on falls into line under him and so on.

But I must add that I would never introduce a new adult male into an established pack and I doubt if this would be acceptable among many stud dogs. Some would mix readily on neutral ground, but they would not willingly accept a strange dog into their home surroundings.

BETTY PENN-BULL

I cannot think of anyone in the world of dogs more capable of writing on the subject of breeding stock than Miss Betty Penn-Bull. Since she can remember Betty has always been immensely interested in dogs. Her literary background enables her to pass on her knowledge in an extremely readable way. Miss Penn-Bull's over-riding desire as a child was to own a dog, but she was never allowed one. Her ambition as a youngster was to make a career with dogs but this too received no support from her family and without any backing she proudly secured her first job aged seventeen. Betty was not able to count on any paid training. It included helping in the house to compensate for lack of experience. After eight kennel jobs gaining experience and having managed to save £35 to start her own kennels, she was fortunate in finding a stable for the equivalent of 25p per week. Single-handed and making every penny count, with trimming, puppy sales, breeding and the use of stud dogs, Miss Penn-Bull built up a strain of Kennelgarth Scottish Terriers who are second to none in the breed here in Britain and anywhere in the world where pedigree dogs are known. Miss Penn-Bull has, since these early days, never been away from dogs and dog shows. She has owned seventeen British champions and bred nine. Betty's home-bred Scottish Terrier Champion Kennelgarth Viking is the greatest top sire ever known, creating a record by siring twenty-three British champions.

J.C.

6 The Labrador in the Field
BY JOE CARTLEDGE

Over the last century the Labrador Retriever has gradually made such a name for itself as a worker both on land and especially in water that it has become easily the most popular and most used shooting dog.

Carefully bred so that their strong retrieving instinct and excellent nose were retained and indeed enhanced, Labradors proved exceptionally useful when to drive pheasant and duck became the usual method of shooting reared birds. Their noses were so keen that they could follow a wounded bird through a covert full of unshot game, and could pursue a wounded duck among decoy birds and such distractions as call-duck and waterhens. With careful selection and training, they also started to make their name respected at field trials as well as in the shooting field.

By about 1911 Labradors were starting to oust the more usual English shooting dog, the Flatcoat, and after the First World War they took control of the shooting field, the field trials and the wild-fowling scene, great numbers being bred for work. Parallel with the present-day popularity of the Labrador as companion and house-dog, numbers of working dogs are still being bred annually. At any shoot there will be half a dozen or so Labradors taking part, with either the keepers or the guns, far outnumbering any other breeds which may be present.

The ideal shooting man's dog, the Labrador should be a strongly built, short-coupled animal, broad and sturdy, still retaining the dense double coat of his Newfoundland hard-weather days. He can be used in many ways, for example, to work covert or to hunt out brambles and hedgerows, so is an excellent rough shooting dog. However, the more orthodox work for which he is trained is either to walk quietly at heel, or sit in a stand while a drive is in progress, 'marking' the fallen birds but doing nothing until he is given the order to go, then collecting the birds as directed and delivering them unharmed into his owner's hand.

For a keen dog it must be torture to have to wait and

watch birds falling and running into the woods without being allowed to collect them until he is told. To do this job, the dog must have the correct cool temperament, be level-headed and obedient, and intelligent enough to watch every bird and keep the tally in his head. Then, when told to go, he must have the self-restraint to look for and retrieve the birds he is directed to by his handler, not running haywire all over the ground, picking up one bird, seeing another, changing about and generally making a nuisance of himself. Besides this level-headedness, he must still have the strong Labrador instincts and attributes: a keen nose, concentration, willingness to oblige, a tender mouth, so that the bird is uncrushed on arrival, and the open-heartedness to come up willingly to his handler and hand over the bird, giving it up without any reluctance.

All these attributes are born in the Labrador if he is

correctly bred, but they can be singularly lacking if the working side of the breed is not carefully fostered and thoroughly tested in the field, generation after generation. It is no good thinking that just because your Labrador isn't good enough for the show ring and likes hunting after rabbit scents he will make a good worker. He may have the hunting instinct and the necessary nose, and also show speed and style, but these are only some of the requirements, and the attributes of willingness, keenness to learn, self-restraint and control, intelligence, tender mouth and game sense do not arise by chance. Without expert breeding they could very soon be lost.

When a Labrador is the right sort (see end of chapter), of sound build and sound mind, he can be trained by a good dog-handler without any difficulty and can prove a most useful companion for the ordinary shooting man. Rear your puppy with plenty of good food and attention. The basic training consists of learning that 'No' means 'No' and not 'Any time you like', that he must walk on a lead without pulling and without carrying the lead in his mouth (a most annoying habit and one that has to be eradicated before dummy-training starts, otherwise the dog, when sent for a dummy, while wearing a light cord during his early training, picks up the cord instead of the dummy). He must, above all, come to you as soon as you call him and must learn to follow you and turn when you turn, keeping his eye on you and trying hard all the time to keep you in sight.

Field Training—Early Stages
The training should begin when the permanent teeth are properly through, so that the puppy doesn't suffer from toothache during training, or catch and pull a loose tooth in his dummy, thus hurting himself and thinking it is the dummy that has caused the pain.

He should learn in very easy stages and in very short lessons. Never keep him at it too long or repeat an exercise too often. See he gets the exercise right, and then leave him with the taste of success in his mouth, so that every lesson ends in praise. A young puppy in training

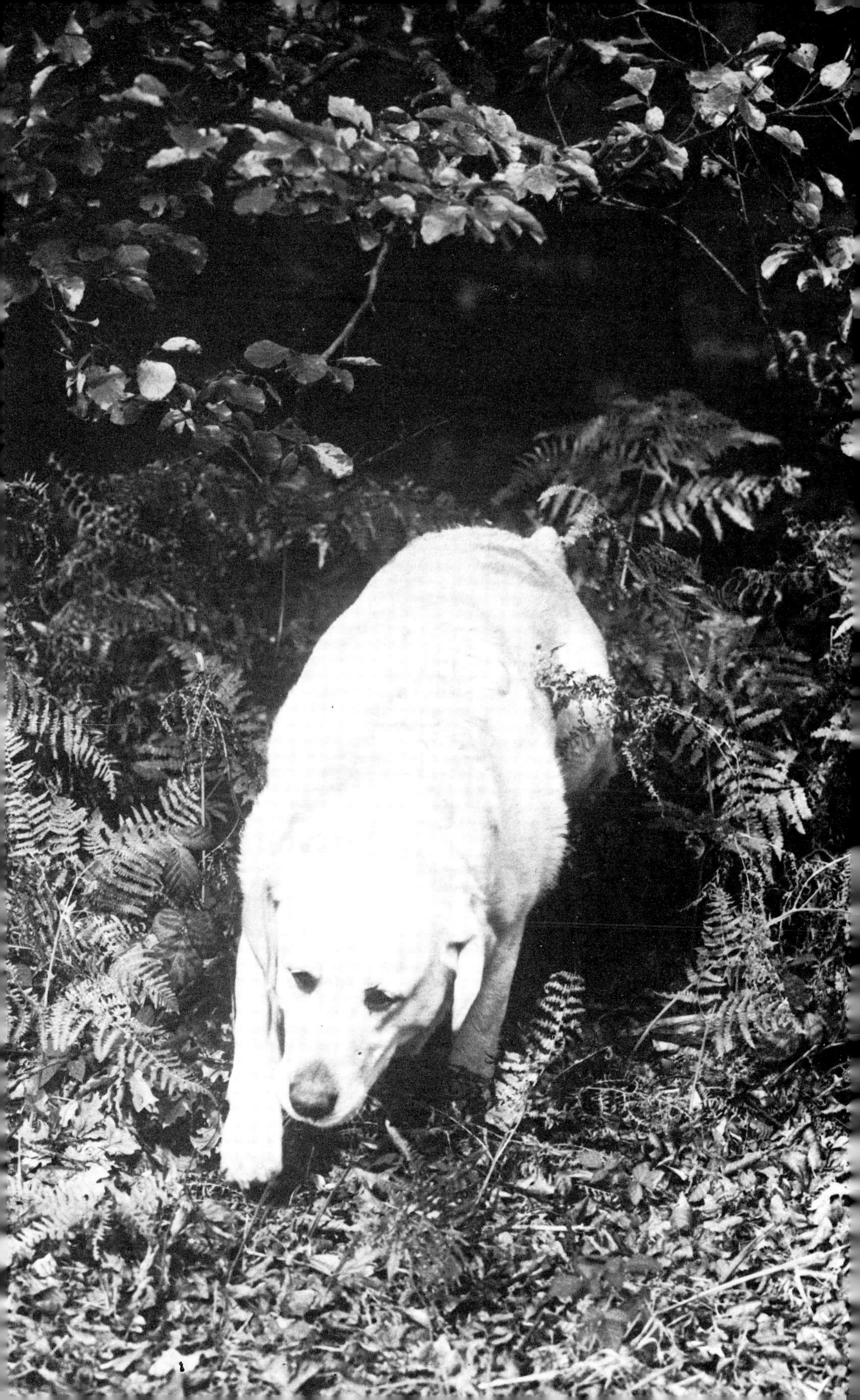

must never feel a failure and never end on a bad or unsuccessful note. If he does fail or if he gets muddled, then don't press the point. Take him back one or two steps in his training to an exercise which you know he fully understands and let him end with that, so that he goes back into his kennel happy, feeling that he did right in the end. This simple point is of vital importance.

The actual retrieve usually presents little difficulty in a well-bred Labrador with strongly developed hereditary working instincts. He will nearly always pick up his first dummy, which should be thrown in the open so that he can run right up to it and pick it up almost before he thinks. The great thing is to have placed yourself so that you intercept him as he runs back with it towards his kennel. This takes a little contriving, but every retrieve has to be a contrived retrieve for the first few months, because the handler must be in complete control of the situation. It is up to you to foresee and anticipate every single thing that occurs during the real training—both the happening and the dog's reaction. Anticipation is in fact one of the keys to successful training. You must learn to know your puppy inside out and to foresee exactly how his mind will work, then you must act more quickly than he does.

After the first successful retrieve of a dummy, you will take your puppy through a series of carefully graded steps, which can be found in any book on gundog training and which are exactly the same for any breed of Retriever (although not the same as the training for a Spaniel, Pointer or Setter, whose jobs are totally different). You can follow the steps easily enough, but remember at all times that every puppy is different and that you must anticipate (that word again!) your puppy's individual and personal reactions. No one and no book can tell you how your own particular animal will behave, so you must be flexible and deal with each situation as you think best, along the general guide-lines laid down in your training manual—or by your own experience, as you get more adept at training.

In the Field
The changeover from training to the actual work in the

field is a very delicate operation, needing due thought and planning. The dog must have been carefully introduced to gunfire, on a fine, clear day, in the open where the shot will not echo. Two people are essential, one to put the dog through a retrieve and one to fire the shot while he is occupied. The man with the gun should stand a good distance away and should turn the gun well away from the dog; he should fire down-wind from the dog, so that the sound travels away. The shot is usually fired after the dog has been sent for the dummy, preferably just as he sees the dummy on the ground and is accelerating and reaching down to pick it up at full gallop. His mind will be on the dummy, and while he may start at the shot and draw back, he will usually turn back to the dummy, which he can see within reach, and will complete the retrieve.

When he does get into the field, your main temptation will be to do too much with him; perhaps you give him one carefully selected bird to retrieve and he does it right, so you then send him for bird after bird. This is fatal. Eventually he starts messing about with them, playing and mouthing them, perhaps tossing them up and plucking feathers out.

This is always a sign that you have done too much too fast. The first few days of shooting can make or mar a dog, so give only one or two carefully selected birds during the day and no more. If these are retrieved correctly, then a small step further may be taken the next shooting day. If all does not go off well, then give less retrieving next time, or take a step back in his training at home to get the fault right. But the one thing to keep always in mind is to end with a success, so don't press your luck by trying it just once again until things go wrong.

Take the greatest care in the choice of game offered the dog for his first real retrieve. He has been used to dummies made of wool or canvas, very often with a pheasant wing or dried rabbit-skin attached to them to give the feel of the real thing. Now, however, he is going to pick his first real 'body', and this is a very different, sometimes exciting and sometimes revolting thing. The very first retrieve on the real thing must be done at home with cold game, not freshly shot, but on no account must it be stale, nor taken from a deep-freeze. Get hold of a small game bird or alternatively a middle-sized young rabbit (not a tiny one, and on no account a big, rank buck or a milky doe, either of which can cause non-retrieving even in an experienced adult dog). Use it the day after it is shot, first making sure it has not been damaged nor badly shot. Do a normal retrieve with the usual dummy, then after a short interval do the same exercise with the real thing. If the dog hesitates and starts to mouth the bird or rabbit, run away towards the kennel yourself to get the dog to dash after you. He will nearly always then pick up the bird or rabbit and follow, and you can take the retrieve as usual.

When he is under fair control, is not gunshy and will retrieve cold game, then you can start him in the field. But remember that a warm, freshly shot bird with blood on it is a different thing from cold game, so ensure that the first retrieve is carefully contrived so that you know he can do it as a continuation of his lessons.

The following birds can be used for first retrieves: partridge, grouse, a small hen pheasant or a very small

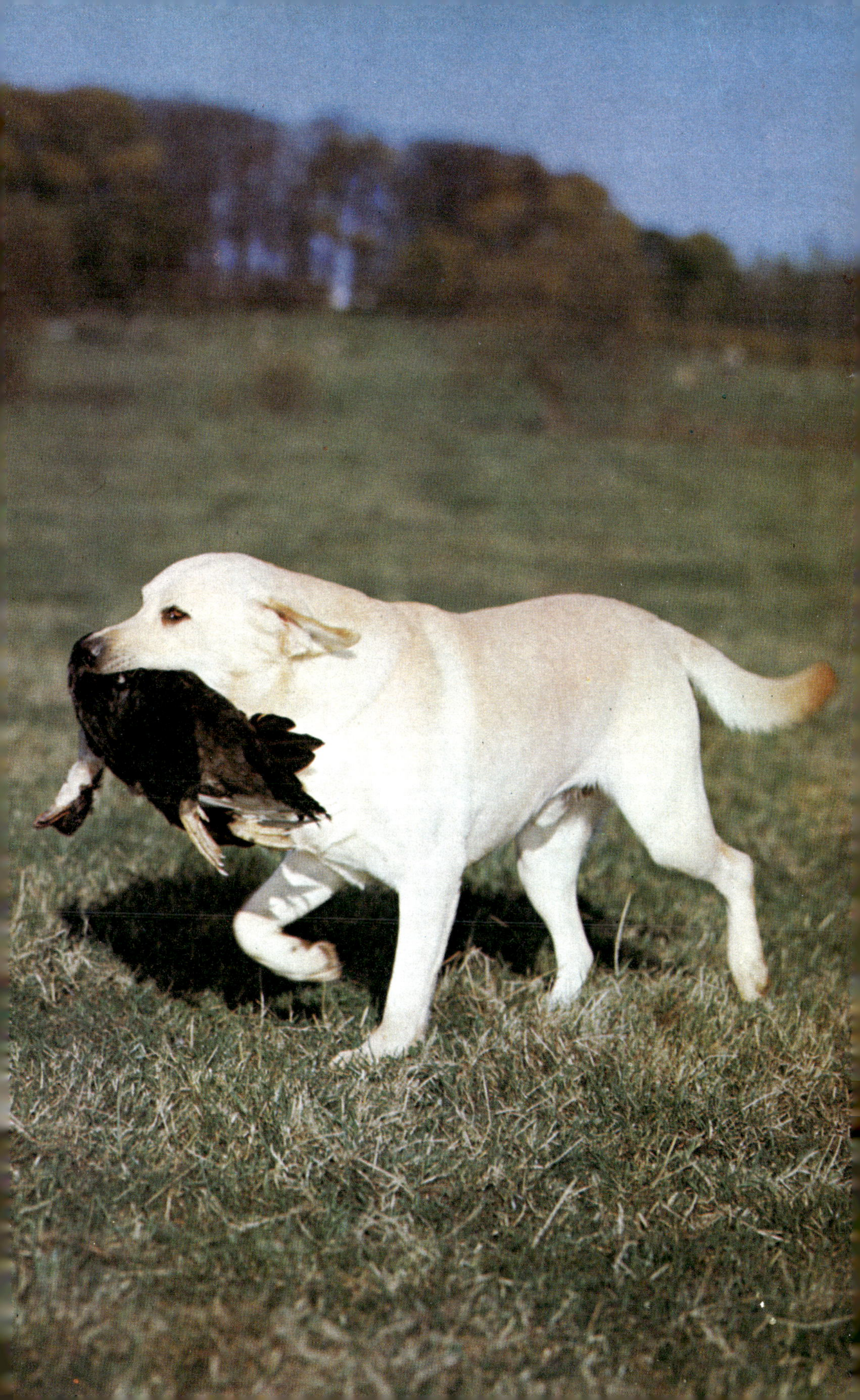

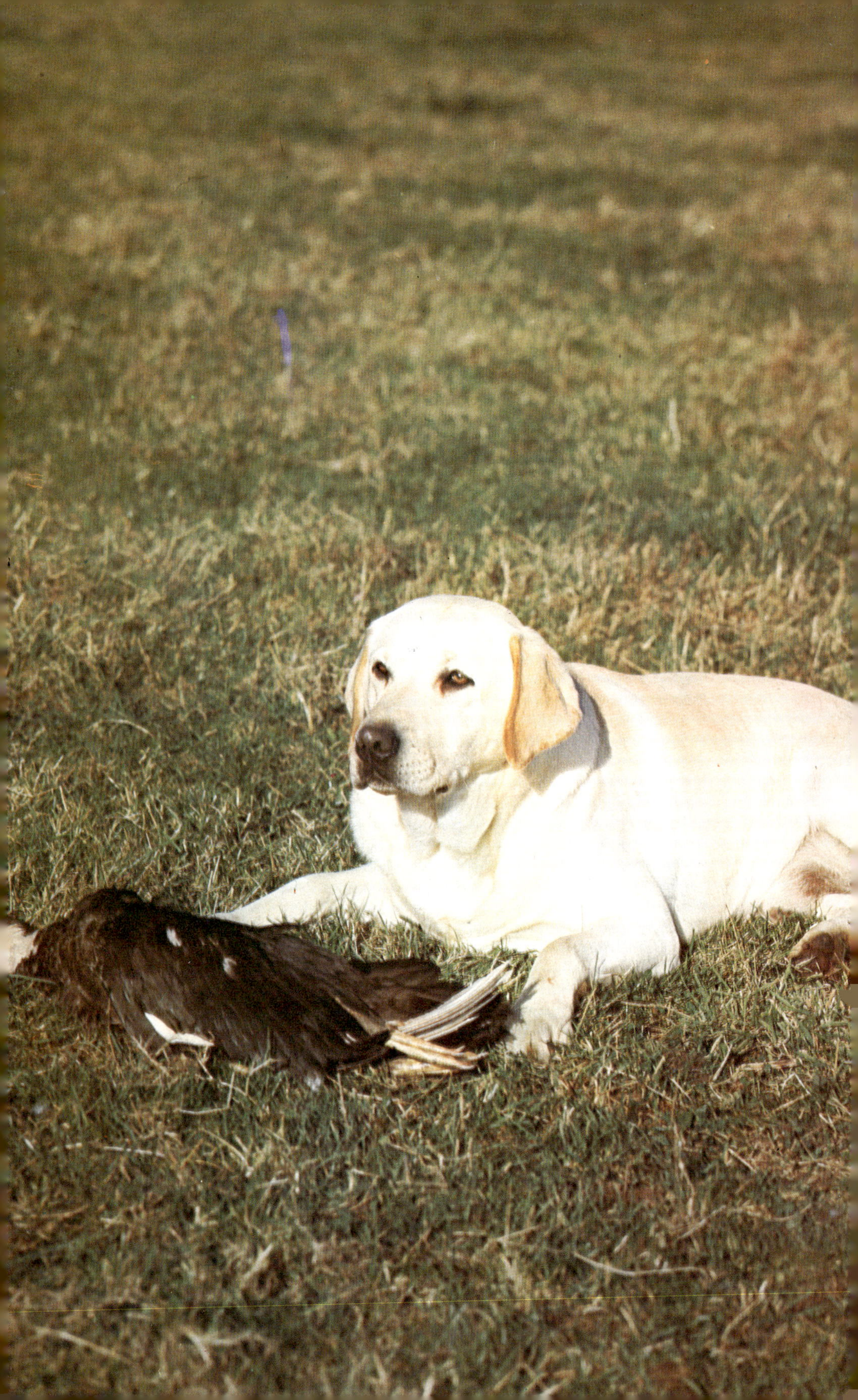

cock pheasant, or alternatively a medium-sized rabbit. The following are *not* suitable for first retrieves and should never be offered until the dog is really good at retrieving and has had some experience: woodcock, duck, moorhens or sawbills, hares, pigeons (unless they are wrapped up in a stocking or handkerchief to prevent the feathers coming out and putting the dog off retrieving for life). Snipe must not be used, nor any form of owl, crow or jay.

The next great danger with the young raw dog is when he gets keen and starts to have a slight grasp of what is happening at a shoot. Here many handling mistakes are made, dogs are ruined in a moment and weeks of careful preparation all thrown away. Don't give your dog too much work—he doesn't need it, contrary to general opinion. He wants less work—to see you yourself pick a dead bird, not him; to be allowed to pick only one selected bird and to see you pick the rest by hand. It is usually too much retrieving that spoils a young dog, not too little. One good retrieve done correctly lasts in his memory for a week or more, and he will come out again the better for it. Eight or more are ruinous. Sooner or later he will start tossing them about and changing birds, if not plucking them or, worse still, eating one.

Give him little to do, but make sure it's done correctly, and get him to progress slowly but surely during his first season. If you want a steady dog, don't let him dash off after a 'runner' in the middle of a drive. He will get right out of hand and dash hither and thither, catching birds as they fall and changing birds all the time, often ending up by galloping after a gliding bird into your host's next drive. Keep him under control until the drive is over, ask your next-door gun or the 'picker-up' to pick that runner if it is still on safe ground, and give your dog one or two carefully selected birds only. This will pay you in his second season, when he can really get down to work and gain experience.

A big risk arises in the first few days of the second shooting season. Your Labrador will remember the joys of shooting, will know he is going to retrieve birds and will 'try it out' by being unruly and unsteady at first, trying to run in and generally show his prowess and strength of working instinct. Keep him under good control for the first few days and he will then settle down to work, and should be by the end of his second season a most useful, experienced and biddable dog.

Working in Water
The Labrador is excellent in this sphere. The average Labrador is mad keen on water once he has been introduced to it; indeed, many puppies just rush into the water and swim like little otters immediately and without any prompting. Their shape is fine for water, being strong and sturdy with very strong legs and good-sized feet in proportion to the bone. The tail also helps the dog in water, especially when he turns with a bird in his mouth, for it both balances him and at the same time acts as a rudder.

   If you want your dog to swim, he should be started young, needless to say in warm weather, and he should be persuaded in, not slung in by force. A biscuit thrown into very shallow water will get him to wet his feet; the next bit of biscuit should be in deeper water, until he is nearly over-balancing to reach it. It is usually then possible to get him just out of his depth, and once he has taken a stroke or two it is very surprising how soon he is swimming as though he had been doing it all his life. He should be started on proper water work at the same time as he is doing his land-dummy work, and the drill is much the same. He must be taught steadiness, so that he does not dash in as soon as the dummy hits the water. He must be taught to turn and swim straight back to you, and should as usual bring the dummy right up to your hand. As he gets keen he can do the exercises you teach him in his ordinary training; sometimes you will send him for a dummy far out that he can see, sometimes for one which has been hidden or thrown when he is not there, and

sometimes you will throw two dummies and then tell him to fetch one of the two.

Choice of a Working Labrador
The colour of a shooting dog is to a certain extent a matter of preference. There are good shooting dogs of all colours, black, yellow and liver (or chocolate, as they have come to be called). Some suit some trainers, some others. There are very good yellow working strains which can take on the very best blacks in the field, but the larger proportion of Labradors used in the shooting field and in field trials are blacks. Since trainers don't bother overmuch with dogs they don't consider suitable, the preponderance of blacks in the field suggests suitability linked to colour. A good yellow can be just as good as a good black, but I have it from a very reliable source that there are more top-class blacks than yellows in the fields, especially at trials. The yellows which do seem to excel have nearly always been of the same few famous working strains, bred by a handful of dedicated trainers. These people have bred yellows for work for many years, and their particular strains have all the necessary good points. At the moment yellows are bred

in great numbers as pets, companions and show dogs and many, sadly, are bred without a thought for the working side. Funnily enough, this does not seem to apply to blacks: the majority of blacks are in working or dual-purpose use. As to chocolates, these are rare indeed in the field, but when they have appeared they have worked well. No conclusion can be drawn from such a small 'sample'. It therefore does not seem to matter much which colour you pick, provided you go to a good working strain.

Size is again a matter of personal preference. The individual shooting man knows what sort of ground he shoots over, the type of fence to be jumped, whether the shoot lies on flat ground and consists entirely of driven birds or whether it is in wall country with thick heather, and situated entirely on high ground, where the guns may be taken up on to the moor in crowded Land Rovers. The wildfowler may like a big dog for a strong tide, the rough shooter may want a small dog for creeping through the hedge-bottoms and brambles. It is no use using a huge Labrador dog if it stops your getting lifts up to the butts, and it's equally no use getting a miniature-sized Labrador if you have to gather your birds over huge boundary walls.

The normal run of size in Labradors is about the Kennel Club Standard, 21½ to 22½ inches, measured from top of shoulder to the ground, but puppies vary in every litter, and strains vary according to their breeder's personal requirements, so you should be able to get the size you desire. Breeders tend to specialise, so find out which kennels breed the colour and size of working dog you have in mind.

Another factor to consider is the sex of the animal. Most shooting men prefer dogs, because the shooting season falls exactly at the time when bitches tend to come on heat, in autumn. A bitch will therefore miss at the very least three weeks of each shooting season. On the other hand, bitches are more confiding in their nature than dogs and therefore easier to control and keep close to your heel. With a dog, while you don't lose time as with a bitch, you do have a different snag, and that is that the dog is always on the lookout for bitches and can therefore be a nuisance on every shooting day, as only half his mind is on the job and the other half on any bitch that may be present.

Most trial handlers far prefer dogs to bitches if they are doing the rounds of the field trials. A very large sum of money may be laid out in fees at the beginning of the trial season, and a bitch who comes into season on October 1st could lose £40 or £50 without having a run to show for it. However, the choice of sex, like that of colour and size, is the buyer's alone. Select the right breeder and make sure the parents are both really useful, sensible, sound and good-tempered, and able to work well, and then pick a puppy that is cheerful and bright-looking.

Classes

There are Labrador clubs covering every part of England and Scotland. Most of these run gun-training classes, so it is usually possible to get your dog to classes which help him in water, or get him used to other dogs taking their turn at retrieving, which is particularly important in water work, where the splash is an almost irresistible temptation to a keen Labrador.

Well-run training classes are very valuable indeed to

amateur handlers. Very often the session ends with tests on dummies, but although such tests are admirable in allowing a trainer to see how his dog has progressed when on fresh ground and under 'surprise' conditions, they are only a practice ground for the real task of a Labrador, which is gundog work in the actual shooting field, with natural game: only on game can the dog be really tested, and this is the job in life for which he is bred.

Note: In writing this chapter on Labradors in the field I am well aware that there are many more capable than I of undertaking such a task. But the recognised experts in the field are not easy to pin down to writing—in fact, I have found it impossible. However, I must add that I have received considerable help from all manner of experts— working dog owners, trainers, and game-keepers. For one reason or another these people wish to remain anonymous, but I must thank them one and all. It would, I feel, be more honest to say that this chapter was written by some of the greatest British working gundog experts, and 'ghosted' by me.

J.C.

7 The Labrador as Guide Dog for the Blind BY LIZ CARTLEDGE

Until the early 50's it was unusual to see a Labrador Retriever in the rôle of guide dog, largely because the German Shepherd (Alsatian) was the dog considered most suitable for the purpose. In fact, during that period the Alsatian was the breed considered most suitable for any kind of training. However, as the demand for guide dogs grew, it became increasingly difficult to obtain sufficient Alsatians of the correct temperament, particularly since more and more of that breed were being used by the police and security firms. Also, at this time a great number of blind people were taking up employment in industry and commerce and required a more socially acceptable dog, which they could take to their place of work. Over the years since the 50's the Labrador has proved to be the most adaptable breed and has shown many good qualities needed in a dog for a blind person to deal with. Friendly by nature, he has a steady walking pace and is less affected than other breeds by the noisy conditions found in large cities, factories and offices. The Labrador has the right body sensitivity for acceptance of harness, and is not unduly affected by a person who may have a slightly uneven walking gait. He is suitable for a much wider range of people than is the Alsatian, making the matching up of dog and handler much easier. The breed also has far less of the chasing instinct found in other types.

The Labrador's only disadvantage for guide dog training is its insatiable appetite. Although all blind people who have guide dogs are advised on the correct feeding for the animal, there is little doubt that the appealing expression of the Labrador directed at other members of the family and the general public results in people being easily persuaded to give the guide dog illicit tit-bits, thinking this is a reward for the great and tireless duty they perform.

'Braille made the blind person literate; the guide dog made him mobile'. Over the past forty years hundreds of blind people have achieved mobility and much independence with the aid of a guide dog, and there is no

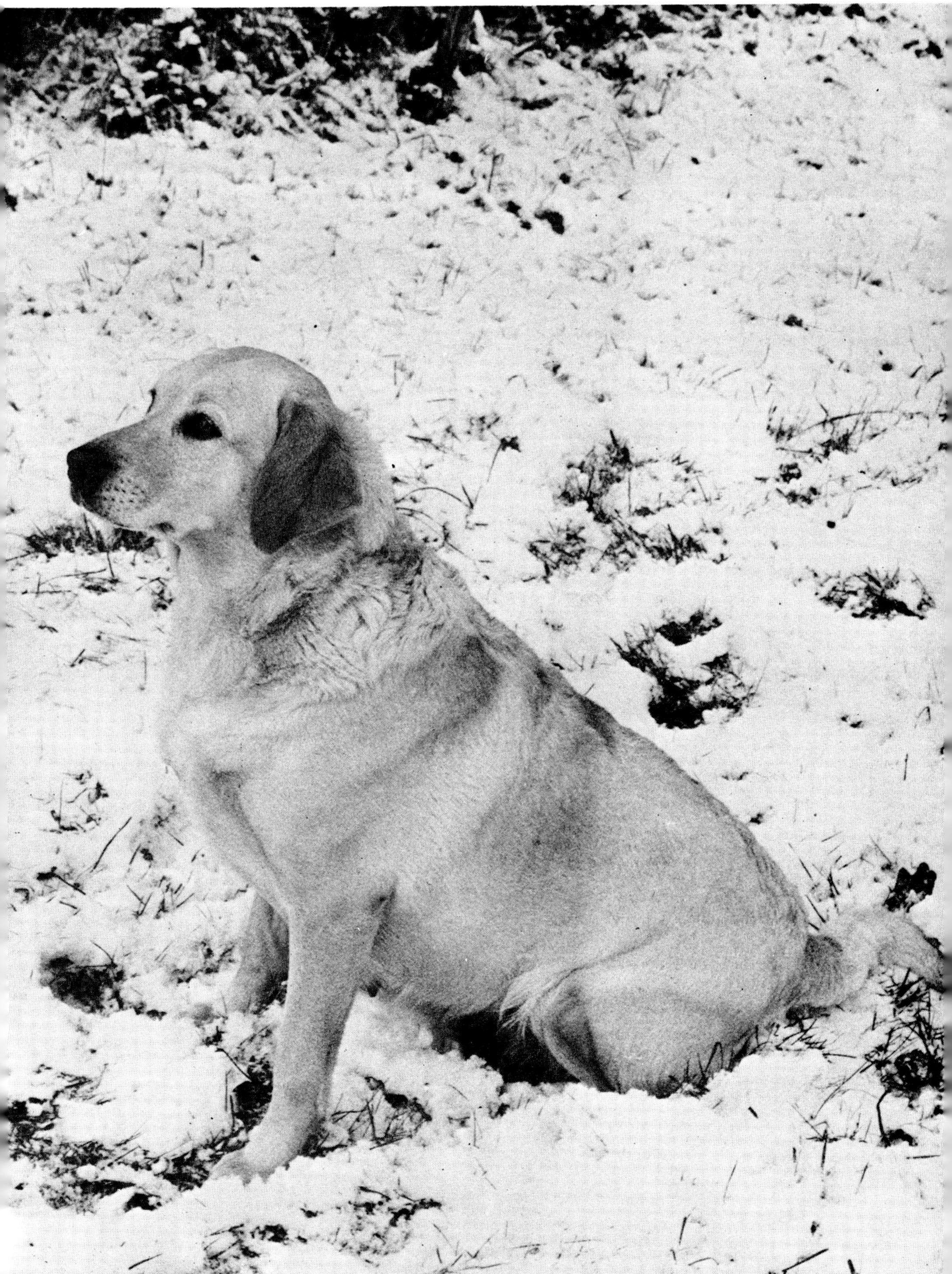

adequate way fully to explain the great work these dogs perform.

Equally praiseworthy is the devoted work done in training the dogs in the centres at Bolton, Exeter, Forfar and Leamington Spa. The training of a guide dog takes about five months.

In recent years, a breeding and puppy-walking centre has also been established, so that the Guide Dogs for the Blind Association can breed its own puppies and provide a regular supply of dogs for the training centres. (The Association is of course the registered charitable organisation which trains the guide dogs and blind persons in their use; it is entirely dependent on the public for financial support.)

About 85 per cent of the dogs used in Britain are Labradors, either black or yellow. But although this is a book on the Labrador, it must be said that good service is also obtained from the Alsatians, the Golden Retrievers and occasionally the Border Collies and the Boxers which are used. Certain crosses of all these breeds are also acceptable, provided they meet the physical and temperamental requirements. About 90 per cent of the animals used are bitches, as it is found they are less dominant than the males and less easily distracted by other dogs. The Association now obtains most of its stock from the breeding and puppy kennels at Tollgate House near Warwick, and at present about 65 per cent of the guide dogs in training have been bred and reared under these arrangements. Puppies are also purchased from reputable breeders, or accepted as gifts, providing they have the right physique and temperament. Adult bitches between the ages of one and two-and-a-half years are also acceptable from the breeds mentioned. These dogs are taken on approval for a period of three weeks and are returned to the owners if unsuitable. In the case of puppies, when they are between six and eight weeks old—that is, if they are so far suitable for the job—they are boarded out in homes and with families living within reasonable distance of the training centres. The family must live in a built-up area, and the puppy should be brought up with children, other household pets, tradesmen and all the noise of urban life. The puppies stay with the 'walkers', as they are called, for about eight months, until they are around ten or twelve months old. The walker must get the puppy used to traffic, going in and out of shops, travelling by public transport, meeting the clatter of trains, in fact, to all the noise and commotion of daily life.

From then on the training of the guide dog lies with the experts, and all through the training period there may be rejections, for over-suspiciousness, too high or too low a degree of body sensitivity, over-possessiveness or bad and unsound temperament. Cat-chasers are definitely excluded! However, thanks to selective breeding, the fall-out rate has decreased considerably over the last few years, and it is hoped that it will drop even further as time goes on and experience is gained.

The Labrador is a magnificent dog in this service for hundreds of blind people, which gives a new outlook and new freedom to those who have all their lives been dependent on other human beings for their every move outside the little circle of their home.

Note: This chapter was written by Liz Cartledge from information given by Mr A. J. Phillipson, Director of Training, and Mr Derek Freeman, Breeding and Puppy-Walking Manager, both of the Guide Dogs for the Blind Association.

8 Common Illnesses

BY MICHAEL STOCKMAN

It is not intended that this chapter should do anything other than describe what a healthy dog should look like and what steps should be taken if any definite change in that state of health should appear. It must be stressed that your veterinary surgeon is there to be consulted on any occasion where the trouble is outside the scope of your own capabilities and delay in obtaining professional advice may result in a worsening of symptoms and a more serious illness arising.

Before one can decide whether or not a dog is ill, it is first necessary to know the classic signs of health. In brief terms these are as follows:

 a Bright, clear eyes.
 b A healthy shining coat.
 c A readiness for exercise.
 d A good appetite.
 e The passage of normal quantities of urine and droppings of normal consistency and colour.

Against this may be listed the signs of abnormality:

 a Dullness of either eyes or coat.
 b Lethargy.
 c Lack of appetite.
 d Excessive thirst.
 e Excessive scratching.
 f Vomiting, diarrhoea and excessive urination.

It is obviously impossible in a single chapter to deal with any but a few of the main problems associated with disease and this I intend to do in alphabetical series.

Accidents

These are usually associated with a painful collision with a car or vehicle, but may be the result of being kicked by a horse. Another accident is the scalded or burnt dog. All these should be examined by your veterinary surgeon as soon as possible and if it is necessary to move a heavy dog it is often possible to carry him on a large blanket. This will not only make the problem of weight much easier to cope with but will also keep the injured animal warm and

help to guard against shock. While on the subject of
accidents, it is well to mention that the dog in pain may
well react to human attempts to assist by biting. That the
helping hand may be the one that normally feeds him is no
guarantee of immunity, so approach the injured dog with
care. If possible apply a stout leather collar and hold on to
it while moving or examining the patient.

Allergies
Many proteins can give rise to allergic reactions which
manifest themselves in general by swellings appearing in
the skin especially round the face. These symptoms are
often referred to under the name of 'nettle-rash' and in
most cases disappear as quickly as they arise, usually
without treatment. Occasionally it is necessary to give an
injection of an anti-histamine drug to counteract the
histamine which has caused the allergy.

The cause may be something the dog has eaten, a sting
from a bee or wasp or even a vaccine injection. Whatever
the reason it is possible that more serious symptoms may
arise as a result of the allergic reaction taking place in the
lining of the stomach or intestine giving rise to vomiting,
diarrhoea or dysentery with passage of blood with loose
faeces. Reactions may also take place in the respiratory
system producing signs of asthma-type breathing. Both
these latter conditions are extremely serious and need very
urgent attention from the veterinary surgeon. It cannot be
too often stressed that when some urgent condition is
apparent it is normally much better to put the patient in
the car and drive straight to the nearest surgery rather
than waiting for a veterinary surgeon to be contacted on
the phone and directed to you. With the advent of multi-
man practices running modern hospitals, all the necessary
equipment is there to deal with an acute emergency.

Anal Glands
These are two secretory sacs lying just below and to either
side of the anal opening. They produce a vile-smelling
protective secretion which in the wild dog presumably
acted as a lubricant to the hard excreta formed by a dog

which ate the skin and bones of its prey as well as the softer flesh. With softer present-day intake our dogs tend to pass a softer motion and as a result the glands' function is partially lost. This causes the sacs to fill up and stretch the overlying tissue, causing the dog discomfort and making him attempt to get relief by rubbing his bottom on the ground or chewing at his hind-quarters with resultant patches of wet eczema on the skin of the area. The cure in simple cases is by digital compression of the glands and most veterinary surgeons if asked will demonstrate the technique. If the later stages of eczema or abscessing have been reached the appropriate professional advice will have to be sought.

Bladder
The urinary bladder, as its name implies, stores the urine. Problems in this organ can be those of inflammation or cystitis with or without bacterial infection, stone-formation within the urine leading to either irritation or blockage of the outlet or urethra, or both conditions together. Correction of all these conditions is essentially the task of the professional man and, especially in the case of a blockage leading to retention, is urgent in the extreme, requiring a greater or lesser degree of surgical intervention. Cystitis itself may need treatment with bladder antiseptics and antibiotics, as well as adjustment of the diet in order to lessen the chances of recurrences. Urine samples are usually needed to assist in making a positive diagnosis and can easily be obtained from dog and bitch alike if the collection is left to the time at which the animal is most ready to relieve itself. Care should be taken that such samples are collected in dishes and bottles free from all contaminants such as sugar. The actual technique of collection is simplified if an old frying pan is used. In the case of the bitch, give her time to get started before sliding the pan into place, or she may well stop.

Ears
The treatment of inflamed ears is without doubt one of the least understood of all first-aid attention required by dogs.

It would, as a generalisation, be better if owners were to leave sore ears severely alone rather than attempt to put matters right themselves. The only action that I would suggest for 'home-doctoring' is the use of a little warm olive-oil poured into the canal of the ear in order to assist the dog's attempts to remove wax and other matter which tends to accumulate as the body's response to inflammation Any attempt at mechanical cleaning, however gently performed, is almost certain to lead to painful and worsening damage to the highly sensitive lining of the external auditory canal. This in turn makes the dog scratch and rub the ear all the more and transforms the mild case into the chronic. There are so many causes of otitis that a proper examination and diagnosis must be made before effective treatment can be instituted.

Eclampsia
This condition occurs in the nursing bitch as a result of lowering of the calcium levels in the bloodstream. The usual time of appearance is about two to three weeks after whelping when the bitch is producing the greatest quantity of milk, but cases are seen from the last week of pregnancy onwards. The symptoms are characteristic, and include rapid breathing, muscular tremors, progressing to incoordination and collapse. Total loss of consciousness may be rapidly followed in untreated cases by death, and help should be gained with the utmost urgency.

Ecto-parasites
This category includes the four main outside invaders which attack the dog's skin, namely, fleas, lice, mites and ticks. All four are unnecessary and every effort should be made to remove not only the parasites on the body itself but also those which have temporarily detached themselves and are in bedding, kennel-walls and the like. The dog-flea can jump prodigious distances and is not fussy about the species to be used as a host; so it may well land on human skin as well as rabbits, hedgehogs and cats. There are numerous effective products on the market, but it is imperative that whatever is used should be employed exactly

according to the makers' instructions (which will usually include warnings about keeping substances away from the animal's eyes). Incidentally, unless the label mentions cats specifically, it is better to assume that it is NOT safe as cats are notoriously susceptible to parasiticides. Lice do not move about with anything like the rapidity of the flea, tending to crawl slowly if they move at all, but they are equally capable of getting off the dog and hiding in cracks and crevices. They are particularly fond of attaching in the folds of skin at the rear edge of the ears and may well be missed as a cause of the dog scratching at its ears. In the cases of both fleas and lice as well as mites, the best method of dealing with those which are off the dog's body in kennels is to use a blow lamp on all surfaces before carrying out the usual cleaning with disinfectant agents.

Mites are the basic cause of manges. The common sarcoptic mange (scabies) is capable of great resistance to treatment even with the most modern of drugs. It most frequently attacks the areas of skin with least hair on them and these are obviously under the elbows and in the groin. Spread is usually rapid to other parts of the body, and also to human beings. Treatment under veterinary supervision is essential. Demodectic mange is seen most commonly in the short coated breeds and is associated with congenital infection. The body seems to have some degree of natural resistance to the mite and symptoms in the form of bald areas are first seen at times of stress such as teething in the puppy, heat-periods and whelping in the bitch; in other words the moments when the resistance is at its lowest ebb.

Mites are also found in dogs' ears, the otodectic mange mites, and these are much more common as a source of ear irritation than is generally realised. It is usual to find that the origin of the infection is a cat living in the same household, so it is advisable to treat the family cat if your dog is found to have otodects.

Ticks are normally found in dogs exercised in fields and do not normally attach in large numbers. They may be removed by bathing in appropriate insecticides, but should not be removed by physically pulling them from the skin;

a drop of ether may be used to persuade the offender to let go, but as many ticks are found by the dog's eyes, this may not be possible.

Eyes
It is as well to deal with the subject of eyes under two quite separate headings. The first can be dealt with very briefly as it concerns the eye-balls themselves, in other words the actual organs of sight. If at any time it should be suspected that a dog's sight is in any way disturbed or impaired, the animal should be taken as soon as possible to a veterinary surgeon and in many cases to one who specialises in opthalmology. There is no place whatsoever for any attempt at home treatment except in the event of a hot or corrosive substance being poured accidentally onto the surface of the eye. In most cases it is best to wash the eye immediately with warm water rather than trying to make up a physiologically correct solution of saline. Having removed to the best of one's ability the damaging substance, the dog should then be rushed straight to the nearest veterinary surgeon.

The eyelids themselves which enclose the conjunctival sacs around the eyes may well be rubbed or scratched by the dog as a result of inflammation of the conjunctiva (conjunctivitis) and it is amazing how much damage a dog can inflict on itself in this way, and treatment should aim at preventing further injury until professional help can be obtained. Simple bland ointments or eye-washes, suitable for use in human eyes, will be perfectly satisfactory for this purpose, but it is essential that these should only be considered as first-aid methods and no substitute for proper advice and treatment. Eyes are much too easily ruined for life to take any risks by adopting a policy of wait and see.

Fits
Any form of fit is a serious matter to the owner and, although often very rapid in both onset and recovery, is none the less frightening to witness, especially when it is the first time a fit has been observed. While the attack is in progress, the animal is best placed in a confined space to

reduce the chance of self-damage. It is unlikely that a dog undergoing a fit will bite deliberately, but care should be taken in handling on those occasions where some restraint is necessary to avoid damage to the patient and property. Once the fit has ended, a rest in a darkened room is advisable, and meanwhile veterinary attention should be obtained. Different causes of fits can often be distinguished by use of the readings of an electro-encephalograph and such assistance in diagnosis will enable the veterinary surgeon to recommend an appropriate line of treatment or management of the individual.

Haemorrhage
Any bleeding from a cut surface should be controlled as soon as possible without waiting for professional help. Wherever it is practicable a pressure pad should be applied by means of cotton wool and bandages. If the first bandage does not stop the bleeding put another one over the top rather than remove the first. If the bleeding on limbs is severe, a tourniquet may be applied above the wound by means of a bandage put on tightly. This is merely a first-aid technique and veterinary help should be obtained as soon as possible. Tourniquets should not be left on more than ten minutes without being slackened and reapplied nearer the wound if necessary. Other bleeding points such as those on the body should be treated by holding a pad of cotton-wool firmly in contact with the wound for some minutes. Do not keep removing the pad to see how things are going as this may well dislodge the newly formed clots. If a wound needs stitching it needs stitching as soon as possible, so do not wait till tomorrow, get help now!

Heatstroke
Under conditions of extreme heat which are sometimes met with in the backs of cars held up in traffic jams, a dog may well suffer from heatstroke as evidenced by vomiting, rapid breathing, weakness and collapse. The body temperature will rise considerably and treatment must begin immediately. Removal to a cool place is obviously the first step and this should be accompanied by the application of cold

water to the head and body either by pouring it over the dog or by immersing the animal in a bath. As soon as the animal shows signs of recovery he should be encouraged to drink and meantime should be dried.

Kidneys
The functions of the kidneys are bound up with the elimination of body waste from the blood-stream via the urine. The kidney is a highly complicated filter mechanism. Like all specialised tissues, kidney cells once damaged or destroyed do not repair to their full efficiency. Once their function is lost, they are replaced by fibrous tissue which can take no part in the technical task of the kidney. Many old dogs suffer from varying degrees of nephritis or inflammation of the kidney. While much of this nephritis is caused by a specific infection with Leptospira Canicola, a great deal of extra stress is put on the organs by overfeeding, especially with protein, throughout the dog's life. A great number of dogs in 'good homes' are fed with some degree of over generosity. Giving three pounds of raw meat to four-month-old Alsatian puppies does no good to anyone but the butcher, and puts a tremendous strain on those organs which have to digest and remove the excess protein, in particular the liver and kidneys. This process repeated over a lifetime will inevitably cause harm. As in the case of cystitis, a sample of urine will be required for aiding diagnosis and it may well be that the veterinary surgeon will wish to take a blood sample to estimate the degree of damage present. Advice on treatment will attempt to ensure that the dog's diet is so adjusted to put as little strain on the kidneys as possible and various prepared diets are available on the market to achieve this purpose.

Poisoning
No attempt will be made to discuss this subject in any breadth. Suffice to say that any substance which can possibly act as a poison to a dog should be kept out of his way. If this policy fails and any poisonous substances are eaten by a dog, an emetic should be administered as quickly as possible. Washing-soda or a solution of salt and

mustard in water will usually do the trick, but even if vomiting is induced, a veterinary surgeon should be consulted as soon as possible for advice as to what further treatment is needed, if possible taking the packet or its name for his information. If the animal is already seriously affected, it is essential that body warmth be maintained while help is being sought, in order to counteract shock. In this context, blankets and hot-water bottles are commonly used. While on the subject of poisons, it is as well to point out that the commonly held opinion that Warfarin rat poisons are harmless to dogs and cats is entirely wrong.

Skin Diseases
Apart from the ecto-parasitic types mentioned elsewhere, there are numerous forms of skin troubles. These include ringworm and bacterial types as well as a host of non-specific conditions. These are the plague of the average veterinary surgeon's existence, and their diagnosis requires considerable expertise. Do not try home cures unless you are certain that you know precisely what you are dealing with.

Stomach and Intestines
The whole length of the alimentary canal from mouth to anus can be involved in varying combinations of inflammatory disorders. The obvious symptoms are vomiting, diarrhoea, dysentery and constipation. The dog, being a carnivore and having in the wild a tendency to scavenge from the carcasses of dead animals, is fortunate in being provided by nature with great ease in vomiting. If this were not so, the dog would have a poor chance of survival, and in many cases a single spasm of vomiting is nothing out of the ordinary, only a response to a bit of injudicious feeding. In most cases vomiting dogs will tend to drink water to excess and it is advisable to remove unlimited supplies of water from their reach. If boiled water with glucose added (one tablespoonful to a pint) is made available in small repeated quantities most dogs will retain it. If after a short period the dog has stopped vomiting it is then reasonable to offer farinaceous foods in the form of

ordinary semi-sweet human biscuits or sponge-cakes for a day or two. If, however, the vomiting continues when glucose water is tried veterinary attention should be sought.

Diarrhoea may occur as a symptom on its own or, as is often the case, as a sequel to vomiting. Again some basic irritation of the bowel is usually the cause and starvation along with the availability of small amounts of glucose-water will often be sufficient to allow the inflammatory condition to subside of its own accord. If it should continue for more than a day or if blood should appear in either vomit or excreta, veterinary advice is essential. Some forms of acute gastro-enteritis produce a great deal of blood from both ends of the alimentary canal and are occasionally rapidly fatal. Professional help is therefore needed at once, whatever the hour.

Constipation is not normally a problem in the dog which is intelligently fed and exercised. It is usually associated with the ingestion of bones whether deliberately provided or scavenged. It is surprising how often well-meaning neighbours will throw bones over the fence to a dog. The safest rule to follow when feeding bones to a dog is to give nothing other than raw, beef, leg-bones. Cooking removes the gelatine and renders the bones more brittle. These are the sort that splinter and provide ideal fragments to penetrate the bowel and cause fatal peritonitis. When constipation occurs, as evidenced by excessive unproductive straining and sometime vomiting, liquid paraffin is the drug of choice and should be given at the rate of an ounce to a 40 lb dog. If this does not produce a rapid answer, get proper help.

While on the subject of the stomach, mention must be made of that violent emergency, torsion of the stomach and Bloat. The affected dog will show symptoms of acute distress with attempts at vomiting with no result. This is because the twisting of the stomach shuts off the cardiac sphincter at the entrance of the stomach and makes it impossible for the stomach contents to leave the organ in a forward direction. The abdomen becomes rapidly and enormously distended and the dog will very soon collapse. This is possibly the most urgent emergency that can be seen in the dog other than the road accident case, and no time should be lost in getting the animal into the nearest surgery or hospital for immediate remedial steps, preferably getting someone else to telephone ahead and warn that the emergency is on its way.

Throats
The sore throat syndrome may be the result of pharyngitis or tonsillitis, or it may be the result of traumatic damage by sharp bones or needles. One useful way of telling the difference is that dogs with inflamed throats and tonsils will show difficulty swallowing and make gulping movements frequently, while the one with needle stuck in its tongue will in addition paw frantically at its mouth. Either way, get professional attention and never make any attempt to remove needles and the like yourself. You are far more likely to push them on down the throat. Choking may be caused by a dog swallowing a rubber ball which lodges behind the molar teeth and occludes the windpipe. An attempt must be made to remove the object with fingers and by cutting the ball with scissors to deflate it, but this is usually very near impossible. Another common cause is the stick that is thrown for a dog to retrieve. On occasion the stick will land in the ground rather than on it and the dog will run head-on into the other end. This will often result in a nasty wound at the back of the mouth. If this happens, never ignore the occurrence; have the dog examined professionally immediately as, apart from anything else, this accident causes considerable shock to the dog.

Uterus
The bitch's uterus is prone to trouble more frequently than that of other domestic animals. This is a result of the very delicate hormonal balance obtaining in the bitch which causes her to suffer false pregnancies almost as a normal state. Unfortunately the theories that breeding from a bitch will have any effect on her future chances of avoiding

either the changes of false pregnancy or the various forms of inflammation of the uterus (metritis, pyometra), are not founded on fact. The suggestion that bitches which have never had a litter are more prone to pyometra than those that have is based purely on the fact that a greater percentage of bitches are in the former category. Owners contemplating mating their bitches should forget the idea that it is for the bitches' good and think first of whether there is a potential market for the possible puppies or not.

Vaccination

Your own veterinary surgeon will inform you of the course of injections which he or she considers most appropriate for your dog or dogs. The diseases which are normally considered are Distemper, Virus Hepatitis and the Leptospira infections. A course of two injections given at the correct ages will give the best possible chance of conferring immunity, and the best advice is that you should consult your veterinary surgeon not later than when the puppy is eight weeks old. You will also get advice as to the correct timing of booster injections and it is unwise to ignore them.

Worms
Until recent years, the worm problem was confined to those types known as round-worms and tape-worms. Now however, there is an increasing incidence of hook-worms and some evidence of whip-worm. It is obviously important to know for certain which particular type is infesting your dog. For this reason it is important to ask your veterinary surgeon to identify a specimen if you are in any doubt as to what it is. Each type of worm needs a different treatment régime and this will include not only dosing the dog with the appropriate remedy, but also dealing with the possibilities of re-infestation. In the case of puppies suffering from the ubiquitous roundworm it is advisable to dose the dam both before breeding from her and once she has weaned the litter.

Finale
If it appears that throughout these notes I have been leading you and your dogs straight into the consulting-room of your veterinary surgeon, I make no apology. When you own a dog or dogs for the first time make it a policy to find a local veterinary surgeon and consult him or her. After the consultation, follow the advice given. If you do you will soon build up mutual confidence and you will receive credit for any knowledge and expertise you will obviously gain. Knowing when you need help, and knowing when you need it urgently are the two pieces of knowledge which will give you the best chance of keeping your dog healthy. If it is at all possible make a habit of taking your dog to the surgery. Many veterinary practices now run efficient appointment systems and in this way you can see

the person of your choice and get the greatest benefit of the full equipment of the practice.

MICHAEL STOCKMAN
I invited Mr Stockman to write this chapter for many reasons, but mainly because I know that for many years he has been very interested, spent much time, and worked very hard to get breeders and members of the veterinary profession to work together in every possible way for the good of the dog. Mr Stockman qualified from the Royal Veterinary College in 1949, and spent four years in the Royal Army Veterinary Corps in Germany and Malaya training war dogs as guards, patrols, and trackers. The rest of his professional life has been spent in a mixed general practice. He is married to a veterinary surgeon who, in his own words, does all the intelligent work in the practice. He first showed dogs in 1942 by handling for a number of breeders and exhibitors of Golden Retrievers, Irish Setters, and Bulldogs. He bought his first Keeshond in 1946, but only started showing the breed with any purpose in about 1960. Now, however, when business permits, he can be seen at most leading shows around the Keeshond rings.

J.C.

9 Kennel Club Breed Standard

The general appearance should be that of a strongly-built, short-coupled, very active dog, broad in the skull, broad and deep through the chest and ribs, broad and strong over the loins and hindquarters. The coat close, short with dense undercoat and free from feather. The dog must move neither too wide nor too close in front or behind, he must stand and move true all round on legs and feet.

Head and Skull
The skull should be broad with a pronounced stop so that the skull is not in a straight line with the nose. The head should be clean cut without fleshy cheeks. The jaws should be medium length and powerful and free from snipiness. The nose wide and the nostrils well developed.

Eyes
The eyes of medium size expressing intelligence and good temper, should be brown or hazel.

Ears
Should not be large and heavy and should hang close to the head, and set rather far back.

Mouth
Teeth should be sound and strong. The lower teeth just behind but touching the upper.

Neck
Should be clean, strong and powerful and set into well placed shoulders.

Forequarters
The shoulders should be long and sloping. The forelegs well boned and straight from the shoulder to the ground when viewed from either the front or side. The dog must move neither too wide nor too close in front.

Body
The chest must be of good width and depth with well-sprung ribs. The back should be short coupled.

Hindquarters
The loins must be wide and strong with well-turned stifles;

hindquarters well developed and not sloping to the tail. The hocks should be slightly bent and the dog must neither be cow-hocked nor move too wide or too close behind.

Feet
Should be round and compact with well-arched toes and well-developed pads.

Tail
The tail is a distinctive feature of the breed; it should be very thick towards the base, gradually tapering towards the tip, of medium length and practically free from any feathering, but clothed thickly all round with the Labrador's short, thick, dense coat, thus giving that peculiar 'rounded' appearance which has been described as the 'Otter' tail. The tail may be carried gaily, but should not curl over the back.

Coat
The coat is another distinctive feature of the breed, it should be short and dense and without wave with a weather-resisting undercoat and should give a fairly hard feeling to the hand.

Colour
The colour is generally black or yellow—but other whole colours are permitted. The coat should be free from any white markings but a small white spot on the chest is allowable. The coat should be of a whole colour and not of a flecked appearance.

Weight and Size
Desired height for dogs, 22–$22\frac{1}{2}$ inches; bitches, $21\frac{1}{2}$–22 inches.

Faults
Under or overshot mouth; no undercoat; bad action; feathering; snipiness on the head; large or heavy ears; cow-hocked; tail curled over back.

Index

Accidents, 120–121
Allergies, 121
Anal glands, 121–122
Asthma, 121

Bee stings, 121
Bladder, 122
Bleeding, 126
Bloat, 129–130
Breed Standard, 134
Burns, 120

Car sickness, 18
Choking, 130
Colours of coat, 10, 39, 112–113
Conjunctivitis, 125
Constipation, 129
Cryptorchidism, 17–18
Cystitis, 122

Dew claws, 88
Diarrhoea, 129
Diet, 18–20
   Bitches in whelp, 80–81
Dysentery, 128

Ears, 122–123
Eclampsia, 123
Ecto-parasites, 123
Entropion, 16
Exercise, 22
Eyes, 125

Feeding, 18–22
   Bitches in whelp, 80–81
Field training, 102–109
Fits, 125–126
Fleas, 123–124

Gastro-enteritis, 129
Grooming, 22–24
Guide dogs, 116–119

Heatstroke, 126–127
Hip Dysplasia, 16
History of the Breed, 38–47
House training, 60–64

Illness, signs of, 120
Inoculations, 131–132

Kenneling, 33–34
Kidneys, 127

Leptospira Canicola, 127
Lice, 123–124

Mange, 124
Mating, 92–97
Mites, 123–124
Monorchidism, 17–18

Nephritis, 127
Nettle-rash, 121

Parasites, 123–125
Peritonitis, 129
Pharyngitis, 130
Poisoning, 127–128
Progressive Retinal Atrophy, 16–17
Puppies, *see Training chapter*
Pyometra, 131

Skin diseases, 128
Spaying, 76
Stomach and intestines, 128–130
Stud dogs, management, 88–92

Tail docking, 88
Throat diseases, 130
Ticks, 123–125
Training, 48–75
   classes, 73, 114–115

Uterus, 130–131

Vaccination, 131–132
Vomiting, 128

Water, working in, 110–112
Weaning, 87
Weight, 33
Whelping, 81–84
Worming puppies, 87–88
Worms, 132

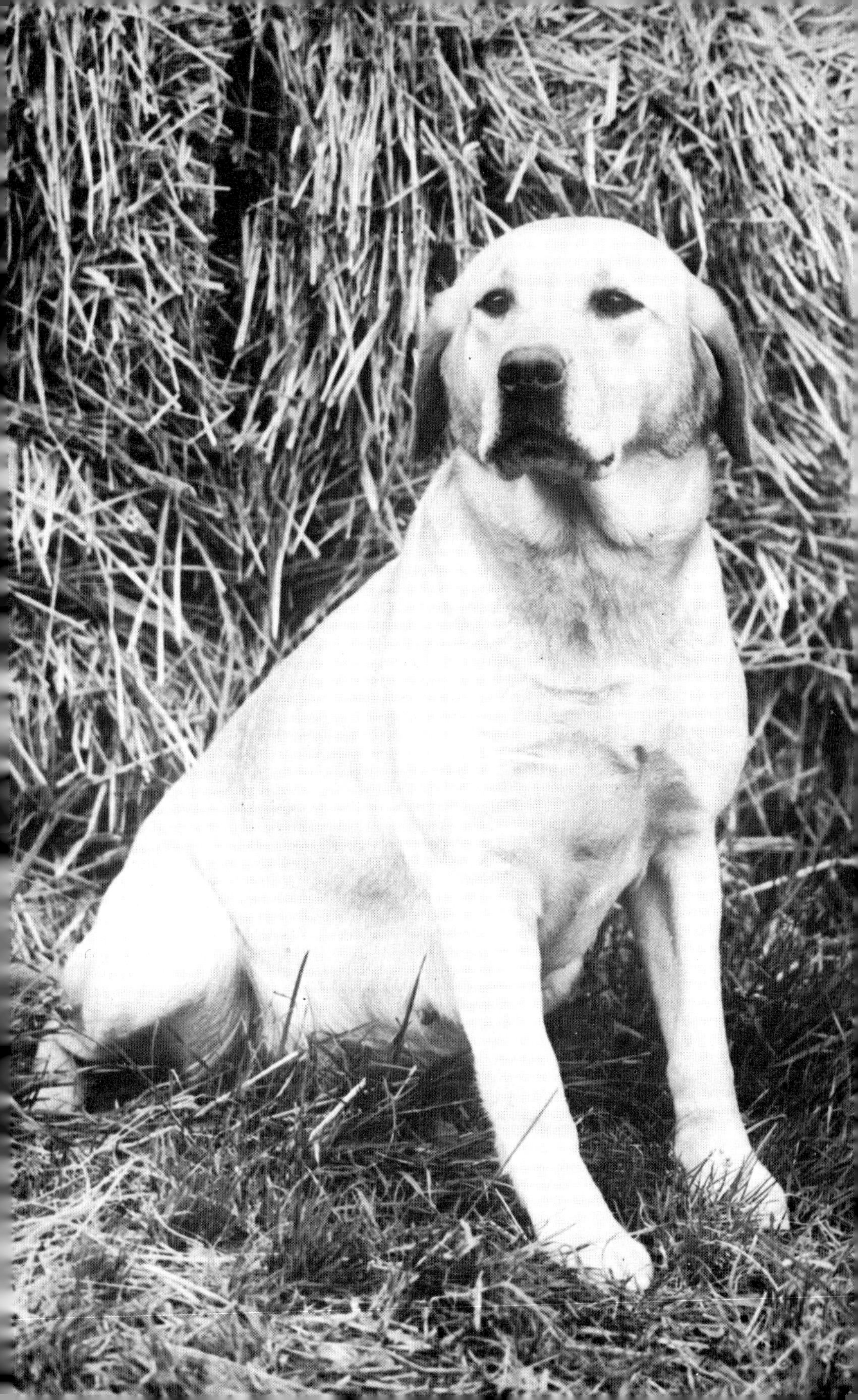